A Pocket Guide to Christian History

A Pocket Guide to Christian History

Kevin O'Donnell

LION

Text copyright © 2009 Kevin O'Donnell
This edition copyright © 2009 Lion Hudson
The author asserts the moral right to be identified as the author of this work

A Lion Book
an imprint of
Lion Hudson plc
Wilkinson House,
Jordan Hill Road,
Oxford OX2 8DR, England
www.lionhudson.com
ISBN 978 0 7459 5287 1 (UK)
ISBN 978 0 8254 6271 9 (US)

Distributed by:
UK: Marston Book Services, PO Box 269, Abingdon, Oxon, OX14 4YN
USA: Trafalgar Square Publishing, 814 N. Franklin Street, Chicago, IL 60610 USA
Christian Market: Kregel Publications, PO Box 2607, Grand Rapids,
MI 49501

First edition 2009
10 9 8 7 6 5 4 3 2 1 0

Acknowledgments
pp. 10, 18, 21, 27, 48, 195, 218 scripture quotations taken from the Holy Bible:
New International Version, NIV, copyright © 1973, 1978, 1984 International Bible
Society. Used by permission of Zondervan. The 'NIV' and 'New International
Version' trademarks are registered in the United States Patent and Trademark
Office by International Bible Society.

A catalogue record for this book is available from the British Library

Typeset in Palatino 10/12.5
Printed and bound in Malta

CONTENTS

Introduction

Did Jesus of Nazareth ever intend to found the church? This is a question asked by a number of scholars who seek to investigate the New Testament and unravel the history of Christian origins. The term 'church' is mentioned in only two places in the Gospels, in Matthew 16:18 and Matthew 18:17, twice only on the lips of Jesus. The Aramaic word he would have used meant 'assembly' or 'community'. The Greek word for this is *ecclesia*, which is used throughout the rest of the New Testament for the church. The church was an assembly, a people more than a hierarchy or a building. As there are only two Gospel references some wonder if this was actually from Jesus rather than later redactors. Did Jesus intend to form a church?

Close attention to the rest of his teaching shows a sense of calling a people together. Jesus' twelve disciples symbolize the twelve tribes of Israel; Jesus told parables about shepherds and sheep, or spoke about gathering people under his wing; and he left a communal meal with his followers to remember his name, his works and his very self. This was the eucharist, or the holy communion, as instituted at the Last Supper. Everything suggests that he was forming and calling a people, creating an assembly, although how he envisaged this taking shape is open to debate. Many think that he saw this as a renewed Israel rather than a new religious movement. Whatever Jesus envisaged, something new began. His disciples became 'apostles', a term meaning messengers with delegated authority from their master, and they went out preaching and converting. And so the church, the assembly of believers in Jesus the Christ (Greek for messiah), began.

Christian or church history hereafter might get entangled with politics, personalities and lots of difficult terms in Greek and Latin. Debates might seem obscure and removed from the reality of everyday life – one example is the discussion about what colour of vestments to wear in the Russian Orthodox Church on the eve of the Bolshevik revolution. But there is more to Christian history than that. In this flow of events we see the foundations of the Christian faith laid down, and the struggles to define important doctrines and beliefs that abide today. Things like the great creeds of the church did not appear out of the sky. They were the result of years of discussion, prayer and reflection as orthodox believers contested rival ideas that they believed would have altered the faith as taught by the apostles.

People might wonder why there are so many different churches. Where did all the denominations come from? A basic study of church history will give some answers. Then again, believers might debate how they should move on in the twenty-first century. Looking over their shoulders and understanding where they have come from and what has happened in the past can be a great help.

This Pocket Guide takes you through key events and discussions in Christian history in a series of ten sections. These are not exhaustive; it is too small a book. Rather than attempting to include everything possible, the events have been condensed, selected and edited. There is much more to the story but here you will find a readable overview, designed to help fit the pieces together. Each section ends with a summary of the timeline involved showing key dates, and an 'at a glance' segment recording the major events of the era. At the back of the book there is a short glossary of key terms, some of which have had a pivotal effect on history.

1. After the Apostles – The First Century AD

The Acts of the Apostles, the New Testament account of the rise of the early church, ends with Paul awaiting trial after his appeal to the Roman emperor, a right to which he was entitled as a Roman citizen. All that the text tells us is that 'For two whole years Paul stayed there in his own rented house and welcomed all who came to see him. Boldly and without hindrance he preached the kingdom of God and taught about the Lord Jesus Christ' (Acts 28:30–31). We hear no more of him in the pages of the New Testament, but history reveals that events were to take a turn for the worse in Rome. The earliest 'Christians' were Jews and thus they were under the protection of the empire, as Judaism was tolerated, and exempted from the laws about sacrificing to Caesar or the pagan deities. However the situation altered as the number of Gentile converts increased.

When Rome suffered a tremendous fire in AD 64, the emperor Nero used the Christians as scapegoats. Many were horribly persecuted, being crucified or thrown to the wild beasts. The apostles Peter and Paul were probably martyred during this time.

The Jewish revolt of AD 66–70 ended with the fall of Jerusalem to the Romans in AD 70; Christian operations moved to mainland Europe and toleration wore thin.

Apostles and martyrs

Jesus called twelve men to be his followers (as described in Mark 3:13–19). At first they are referred to as the twelve disciples, from the Latin version of the Greek word *mathētēs* meaning 'learner' or 'student'. Latterly, after the establishment of belief in the resurrection of Jesus, they are known as the apostles.

An apostle was one sent out with authority, an ambassador bearing the seal of the king or emperor. The transition from one to the other is a remarkable detail of Christian history. To some, Jesus seemed to have failed as he was executed on a cross. Most of his disciples fled and deserted him, losing their faith. But something galvanized them, turning them around and renewing their belief. The gospels relate that this event was the resurrection of Jesus, a mysterious, elusive event that is attested in various narratives and is affirmed in the rest of the New Testament as the pivotal event that birthed the church.

The biblical apostles were leaders of the early church, standing in for Jesus, seeing themselves as his delegates. Some of the apostles and early believers were martyrs (from the Greek word *martyrion* meaning 'witness'). One who gave his or her life for the faith was a 'martyr' par excellence, and according to church tradition many of the apostles were martyred, although the only martyrs mentioned in the New Testament were Stephen the deacon (Acts 6–8) and James, the brother of John (Acts 12:2). Nothing is known about the fate of some, but there is a cluster of traditions about other apostles. There is little hard evidence and much that we do not know, as only certain things were written down. After the New Testament there are scattered references in later writings of the church fathers such as Eusebius (c. AD 260–340) who wrote his *Ecclesiastical History* after the emperor Constantine's conversion. However, there are many legends and oral traditions, which probably contain at least some truth. Sometimes these are varied and contradictory, but the list below is a summary of the main traditions about a number of the apostles.

- **Paul** was reportedly beheaded at Rome, during Nero's persecution. This would have been on the Appian Way, leading out of the city. Beheading was the death penalty for a Roman citizen. Alternatively, some have wondered if he was released after his appeal to the emperor and then went as a missionary to southern Spain ('Tarshish' in the Scriptures), as he had mentioned his desire to visit this area, which people at that time saw as 'the ends of the earth'. There is no evidence of this and the Appian Way tradition is more likely.

- **Peter** was, according to tradition, crucified during Nero's persecution. He would have been crucified upside down as he was not worthy to suffer the same fate as his master. Accounts add that the body of Peter was buried in a sarcophagus beneath Vatican Hill close to the place of his martyrdom, in a well-known necropolis, which was marked with a single, red rock. In the fourth century the emperor Constantine ordered the erection of the original basilica of St Peter over this spot. Peter's tomb is venerated beneath the high altar of St Peter's in Rome, the bones being found in an ancient Roman cemetery there.

- **James**, the brother of Jesus,[1] was stoned to death in Jerusalem in AD 62 at the instigation of the Jewish parliament, the Sanhedrin.

- **Matthew** was said to have been martyred but there are rival tales of this taking place in Rome, Ethiopia and Persia.

- **Thomas** was reportedly killed by a spear in India. Thomas has left a trail of veneration through the area of Iraq and along trade routes to India where the Mar Thoma church traces its descent from him. Its members point to a shrine in Madras that bears a seventh-century inscription; they believe that Thomas's body was interred here before being moved to Edessa in Syria.

- **Bartholomew** was said to have been flayed alive and beheaded in India or Armenia.
- **Andrew** was reportedly crucified in Greece.
- **James**, son of Alphaeus, was clubbed to death in AD 62 in Jerusalem.
- **Simon** the Zealot was said to have been martyred with Jude, a brother of Jesus, in Persia.
- **Philip** reputedly died peacefully at Phrygia.
- **John** was exiled to the isle of Patmos and died in old age. If John was 'the beloved disciple' mentioned in the fourth Gospel, then he received Mary the mother of Jesus into his care when Jesus died. They reputedly lived together in a house in Ephesus which is a shrine to this day.

Some wonder what would have happened if the church had gone east rather than west. It did, in part. Besides following the trade routes of the Roman empire across North Africa, into Europe and Rome itself, missionaries found their way into the Persian empire (modern-day Iran and Iraq) and further afield at least as far as India. (Later Christians followed the old silk route into the Far East and China.) However the power of Rome and its widespread empire with an excellent system of communication meant that the church in the West was to have more widespread and lasting influence in history.

The four Gospels – sources of the Christian story

The exact date of the composition of the four Gospels is unknown and is a matter of conjecture by scholars. Certain parameters help us, such as the end of the first century when Clement of Rome quoted from the Sermon on the Mount in Matthew (c. AD 95) and saw these verses as scripture. A fragment of John was found in the sands of Egypt which is dated between AD 110 and 130; allowing time for this to be copied and circulated and to gain authority, it must have been written no later than the end of the first century. Scholars usually suggest the following chart of dates:

c. 65–70	Mark
c. 85–95	Luke and Matthew
c. 95	John

Some have suggested earlier dates, such as Bishop J. A. T. Robinson, who argued that all the Gospels predate AD 70 as none explicitly mention the fall of the Temple in Jerusalem. His views, however, have not been widely accepted. Belief in the testimony of the apostles behind the sayings and narratives in the Gospels has ancient pedigree. Early Christian writers such as the early second-century bishop Papias of Hierapolis argued that Matthew wrote the *logia* (sayings) in the Hebrew tongue rather than in Greek, and that Mark was the interpreter of Peter. Papias also testifies to a living oral tradition that told and retold the stories and the teachings alongside the written books, 'I supposed that things out of books did not profit me so much as the utterances of a voice which lives and abides.'[2] We would do well to remember that the ancients were more adept at oral transmission in a pre-literate culture. One Jewish rabbi said,

'A well-trained pupil is like a well-plastered cistern that loses not a drop.'

The Jews, Rome and the Christians

Persecution was recurrent in the first few centuries of Christianity, and it came firstly from some of the Jewish leaders, who saw the early Christians as troublemakers and heretics. The first Christians were Jews who had no idea of forming a new religion but rather were seeking to fulfil and renew their own. At the time, they would have been seen as one of various messianic groups that came and went. Tensions in Judea meant that the Sanhedrin were afraid of the Romans intervening to put down any revolts as they could be ruthless. The Sanhedrin was suspicious of the new Jesus movement; after all, its founder had been crucified by the Romans as a criminal.

The Jewish revolt of AD 66–70 saw the fall of Jerusalem and the end of the Sanhedrin's power. This might have eased relationships between Jewish followers of Jesus and their co-religionists, but, in fact, some Jewish attitudes to the Christians hardened as the Pharisees survived the fall of Jerusalem and codified traditions and oral laws, defining Judaism for years to come and excluding Christian ideas and versions of Judaism. Also, the flight of Christians from Jerusalem before its fall, when Symeon, the cousin of Jesus, had led them out to the hill town of Pella, had caused mistrust. By the time of the Jewish Council of Jamnia in AD 85, Christians (also called 'Nazarenes') were declared heretics, though some did still attend the synagogues but could take no official role. To make matters worse, Christians saw the destruction of the Holy City as divine judgment.

The Roman persecution of the Christians began with Nero's bloodthirsty attack after the Great Fire of Rome in AD 64 but it was not in evidence again until the end of the first century.

Some argue that their apocalyptic preaching about the end of the world and the fire of God's wrath made them suitable scapegoats for the fire of Rome. The early second-century writers Pliny the Younger and Cornelius Tacitus shed some light on how the believers were seen. Cornelius Tacitus wrote:

> *Christus, from whom the name had its origin, suffered the*
> *extreme penalty during the reign of Tiberius at the hands of one*
> *of our procurators, Pontius Pilate, and a deadly superstition,*
> *thus checked for the moment, again broke out not only in Judaea,*
> *the first source of the evil, but also in the City, where all things*
> *hideous and shameful from every part of the world meet and*
> *become popular.*[3]

Pliny, the governor of Bithynia, in modern-day Turkey, says that they worshipped Christ as a god and that the governor was encouraged not to bother hunting them out unless he was presented with evidence that they were believers. The attitude seemed to be 'Deal with them if you have to, but don't go looking for trouble.'

Persecution returned at the end of the first century and in the early second century along with the practice of sacrificing incense to an image of the emperor as a sign of loyalty. Jews were exempt from this as strict monotheists but Gentile converts to Christianity were not.

Early theology

The first century saw conflicts about how traditionally Jewish the Christian faith should be. This was in a context of varied expressions of Judaism, which became more codified after the fall of Jerusalem. The apostle Paul constantly struggled with the Jewish Christians who wanted his Gentile converts to be circumcised and to follow the Jewish food laws. These opponents are sometimes referred to as the 'Judaizers' but who exactly they were, and who they represented, is open to debate. The account of the Council of Jerusalem in Acts 15 sees Paul gathered with the apostles and with James, the brother of Jesus, to address this matter. A compromise was reached whereby the many ritual food laws and circumcision were not to be forced upon Gentiles, but they were to abstain from blood and meat offered to idols. In a sense, much of the first century of Christianity was about working out just how Jewish Christianity should, or indeed could, be.

Early Jewish Christian theology

During this period, Jesus was seen as the Word or Wisdom of God (John 1:14 and 1 Corinthians 1:24) following the Old Testament use of divine *hypostases*, a Greek term meaning extensions or emanations of God's being, as articulated and praised by Jewish philosophers such as Philo of Alexandria (c. 20 BC–AD 50). These were the Semitic sages of the Diaspora, the network of Jewish communities across the Greco-Roman world. The *hypostases* could be the Wisdom, the Word or the Spirit active in the earth (see Proverbs 8:22–23; Isaiah 55:11; Psalm 104:30 respectively). God was totally outside and beyond the world, but he could step into his creation to influence it. The parts of God that stepped in were like extensions or emanations of his being. Thus a *transcendent* deity had an *immanent* involvement in the world through his emanations, to use theological language. The New Testament saw the Word and Widom as taking flesh in Christ, a novel and controversial theological development. Jesus was also seen as the new Temple and the perfect, atoning sacrifice (see Hebrews 10; John 2:21–22; Ephesians 2:11–22). For the early church Jesus replaced and fulfilled, in his person, the cultic centre and the methods of atoning sacrifice in its ritual.

From this we can see that the central tenet of Christianity was already entrenched; the cross was seen as salvific. Many images and metaphors were used to evoke its saving power, for example images from the slave markets and the sacrificial cult. Jesus redeemed humanity by his blood (from the power of sin, from the wrath of God or from the power of the devil) and his blood was a means of cleansing. Subsequent theologians would debate the nature of this salvation, but the core idea that Jesus took sin upon himself on the cross was a very early one.

Only an appearance?

Later in the first century, there is evidence of a new current that sought to proclaim that Jesus only seemed to be human – that his body was an appearance only – for the divine could not really take flesh. It is combated in the epistles of John, who writes that 'Every spirit that acknowledges that Jesus Christ has come in the flesh is from God... ' (1 John 4:2b). This revisionist view was known as 'docetism' from the Greek word *dokeo* meaning 'to appear'. It was influenced by Greek philosophy from thinkers such as Plato (427–347 BC) and his followers, wherein matter was inferior or even bad and God was high above. This view believed God created the world through a go-between, a demiurge. As the faith spread throughout the Roman world, pagan ideas such as this took root and swayed people from the original, apostolic faith. Christian leaders had to learn a new language with which to explain and defend the gospel.

The early church at worship

The end of the first century saw a separation of church assembly and synagogue worship. For many years believers who were

Jews had attended both. 'Church' was in a private home or room in an apartment block. There were no special buildings as people did not have the means for them, and the periods of persecution had also been prohibitive.[4] Saturday was the Jewish Sabbath, celebrating the creation of the world, and Sunday was the day of the resurrection, celebrating the new creation. Sunday was a working day in the Roman empire and so believers assembled together early in the morning and late in the evening when they shared the *agapē*, a love-feast. Though the day of celebration had been changed, the early Christians took their Jewish roots with them once they began to separate from Judaism, singing psalms and using Old Testament Scriptures.

The selective, secretive gatherings, especially in times of persecution, as well as the 'love-feast', suggested all sorts of scurrilous behaviour to the Romans. Talk of eating the 'body and blood' of Christ in the eucharistic meal of bread and wine even raised charges of secret acts of cannibalism. Officials who actually looked into their behaviour saw that this was not the case, however. Pliny the Younger, for example, wrote of the believers early in the second century: 'They... bind themselves with an oath: not to commit any crime, but to abstain from all acts of theft, robbery and adultery, and from breaches of trust...'.[5]

Baptism

The exhortation in Acts 2:38 is simple: repent, be baptized and receive the Holy Spirit. Peter's message for Christians is clear. What baptismal practice was in the early church, however, is not so plain. It could have been by total immersion or by pouring water over the head. The emergent practice seems to have been a form of partial immersion, in which the recipient would kneel and have water poured over him (the rabbis of the time put pagan converts to Judaism through a ritual bath in a similar way).

A further question relates to infant baptism. There is no definite mention of this in the New Testament although the early church came to believe that this practice was apostolic. There are references made to household baptism; for example, in Acts 16:31 the Philippian jailer's whole family are baptized, but their ages are not mentioned. Infant baptism came to be practised widely in the early church, but not universally for some time (again it may be relevant that converts to Judaism would take infants through the ritual bath with them).

The formula of baptism also developed in this period. References in Acts suggest that this was 'in the name of Jesus', but Trinitarian (that is, in the name of the Father, the Son and the Holy Spirit) baptism became the norm. The end of Matthew's Gospel has the risen Jesus commanding Trinitarian baptism (Matthew 28:19). A remarkable teaching document has been preserved from the end of the first century, entitled *The Didache*, or *The Teaching of the Twelve Apostles*. It is a manual of ethics, church discipline and sacramental practice, and in it baptism is Trinitarian. It specifies that running water or a pool can be used, though if neither is available, water is to be poured three times over the head.

Eucharist

The New Testament tells us very little about the early Christian celebration of the eucharist, the 'thanksgiving' that used bread and wine after the fashion of the Last Supper. There are the narratives of the Last Supper in the first three Gospels and a rich tapestry of eucharistic symbolism in John. John has no description of the Last Supper, yet throughout the weave of his Gospel there are symbols of water, bread and wine. (The custom at the time was to mix wine and water in the cup of blessing at Jewish meals.)

Paul reveals the most about the celebration of the eucharist in 1 Corinthians 11:17–34. He tells the Corinthians to recite the 'dominical words', the institution narrative from the Gospels as spoken by Jesus, 'This is my body... this is my blood.' Paul adds that doing this 'proclaims the Lord's death until he comes'. He also cautions the believers to eat and drink worthily, not selfishly and abiding in sin. The eucharist seems to have been part of an *agapē* love-feast and some of the Corinthians were eating the best food and not sharing it.

The next glimpse of a eucharist is in the first-century document *The Didache*, which also describes the eucharist as a part of an *agapē*. The prayers are closely modelled on the Jewish table graces. First, the wine then the bread is blessed. This is an early variant which takes its cue from the Passover meal itself with different blessings over cups of wine:

> *We give thanks to thee, our Father, for the holy Vine of thy*
> *servant David, which thou hast made known to us through thy*
> *servant Jesus.*
> *We give thanks to thee, our Father, for the life and knowledge*
> *thou hast made known to us through thy servant Jesus.*[6]

There is no institution narrative included – it is probably assumed that this is well known and will be used, but it is strange that it goes unmentioned.

The Lord's Day

The Didache and also later writers such as Justin Martyr (d. AD 165) give us glimpses of a Sunday worship service. All agree that this consisted of the eucharist and took place weekly. *The Didache* links this with Malachi 1:11 and the idea of a pure offering offered all over the world in honour of the Lord. Confession of faults has to precede this offering to make it acceptable. Justin gives the fullest description of the Sunday gathering; in his account it follows the structure of synagogue worship with the eucharist added on. A liturgy of the Word with readings, psalms and teaching includes intercessions and praises, followed by the kiss of peace and the bringing of bread and a mixed chalice of water and wine. Thanksgiving is made over this and the institution narrative repeated so that it becomes holy. Only the baptized may partake.

There is a suggestion of the free participation of some people, of spontaneous and open prayer amongst the liturgy. Thanks can be given freely by the elder, or presbyter, over the bread and wine. It is only later that we clearly have a set eucharistic prayer in use. *The Didache* also speaks of the role of visiting prophets who can give thanks as they please and who can speak oracles and exhortations to the assembly. The worship of the early church had a spontaneous, charismatic dimension, as can be seen in the pages of the New Testament (e.g. 1 Corinthians 14:26 and Ephesians 5:19–20). This charismatic element only gradually faded as the church's ministry became settled and ordered, and liturgy became more exact in order to counter heresies.

Timeline

64	Fire of Rome and Nero's persecution; deaths of Peter and Paul
66–70	Jewish War and the fall of Jerusalem
65–95	Writing of the four Gospels
85	Jewish Council of Jamnia
Late 1st century	Writing of *The Didache*

At a glance

- The church began after belief in the resurrection of Jesus took hold and the disciples were seen as 'apostles', messengers with a mandate from their master.
- Many of the apostles seem to have been martyred in the first century AD as they travelled around the Roman empire, and further east as far as India.
- The first Christians were Jews and enjoyed the protection of Roman law; however as more Gentiles were converted, Christians began to be persecuted for not worshipping the emperor or the pagan gods.
- The four Gospels were in existence by the end of the first century AD. Some verses from these were being used as Scripture by first-century writers.
- The first century saw a struggle for Jewish/Gentile identity in the church over issues such as circumcision and the food laws. Early theology spoke of Jesus as messiah, the fulfilment of the Temple cult, an atonement for sin and the Word made flesh.
- By the close of the century, as the gospel became rooted in the empire, there were new interpretations of Jesus influenced by Greek philosophy such as docetism, whose adherents believed that Jesus only appeared to take flesh.
- The first Christians worshipped in secret, in homes, early in the morning or late in the evening. Baptism could use different forms and formulas, but gradually developed into a Trinitarian form with pourings of water, and increasingly included the infants of committed believers. The eucharist was celebrated as part of an *agapē*, a communal meal, and came to be seen as a fulfilment of Old Testament prophecies about a universal, pure offering to the Lord by all nations.

Endnotes

1. 'Brother' of Jesus might have actually referred to cousin or step-brother, as the Greek word *adelphos* could carry a range of meanings. An early tradition claimed that Joseph was an elderly widower who married Mary to protect her and that Jesus was the youngest child, a step-brother of Joseph's sons and daughters.

2. Eusebius, *The History of the Church*, trans. G. A. Wiliamson, London: Penguin Classics, 1965, p. 152.

3. Tertullian, *A New Eusebius*, ed. J. Stevenson, London: SPCK, 1977, p. 3.

4. As time went on, it seems that sometimes private houses were bought and converted into a primitive form of church. Archaeologists have found evidence of a third-century one in Dura Europos, Syria. This used the main room as the meeting room with the table used for the eucharist. A side room had a baptistery large enough for an adult to kneel down in and to have water poured over them from a large pitcher. Other rooms would have been used for catechesis. There is no evidence of anything as organized or as arranged as this any earlier than the third century – a time which was relatively free of persecution when many openly professed their Christian faith.

5. Pliny the Younger, *The Letters of the Younger Pliny*, trans. Betty Radice, London: Penguin Classics, 1963, p. 294.

6. M. Staniforth, *Early Christian Writings*, London: Penguin Classics, 1987, p. 194.

2. Christ and Hellenism – The Second and Third Centuries

If the first century was concerned with how authentically Jewish the Christian faith should remain, then the second struggled with how Greek it should be, especially in terms of how Jesus was understood. Other issues involved the value of martyrdom and the nature of church authority, both of which were pressurized in a climate of political instability and intolerance. This period saw the formation of the New Testament canon – the approved list of books that should be included in the New Testament Scriptures.

Persecutions, divisions and empire

During the second and third centuries, Roman persecutions were not continuous or systematic; however the Christians received bad press over accusations of secret meetings, supposed cannibalism (i.e. eating the body and blood of their master) and their refusal to sacrifice incense to the emperor as a living deity. They took no part in local, civic celebrations that honoured the pagan gods and thus they were dubbed 'atheists'. These failings in the eyes of Rome (and indeed, the individual dispositions of some emperors) led to a great deal of persecution – if something was wrong in the empire, the Christians were an easy group to blame and, in turn, punish.

The first half of the third century AD was peaceful for the church. Many were used to the 'new movement'. Emperor Alexander Severus included Christ in his pantheon of gods; Emperor Philip the Arab employed many Christians on his staff and was said to be 'almost a Christian'. However, things changed radically with the emperor Decius (205–51) as the mid-point of the century was reached. The Goths were attacking from the west and the Persians from the east. Taxes and inflation were high and riots broke out. The Christians, who were committed pacifists, were scapegoated as they would not join the army and had not taken part in celebratory festivals – they were seen as 'traitors within'.

Church leaders were arrested and others ordered to sacrifice in honour of the emperor or buy certificates saying that they had. Many believers were more relaxed by now and used to a peaceful life – some sacrificed, many bought certificates.

Decius was killed in 251. His successor, the emperor Valerian, started persecutions again in 258, killing many church leaders. The refusal of the growing number of Christians to sacrifice to the pagan gods was seen as a possible reason for the economic and political troubles of the age – the imperial currency was debased to an extraordinary degree and the weakened empire had little patience for rebels.

As a consequence of the actions against the Christians, problems broke out over how to treat those who had lapsed under persecution. After Decius's persecution, Cyprian, Bishop of Carthage (d. 258) argued with Stephen, Bishop of Rome. A breakaway church, the 'Pure Ones', had started, led by Novatian. Should his converts be rebaptized if they joined the Catholic

Church? Cyprian said yes, Stephen no. Novatus, another early Christian teacher, held a third view. He urged total leniency and grace for all the lapsed. However Cyprian and others had lengthy penance for the certificate buyers and only the possibility of death-bed forgiveness for the sacrificers. These were harsh times. When many had paid for their faith by shedding their own blood, after all, feelings ran high and differences of opinion could not easily be dismissed.

The martyrs

The last chapter introduced the reality of martyrdom in the earliest days of the first-century church and the honour such people received. The second century began to see a more formalized way of expressing this respect. The martyrs were honoured as exemplary Christians and their tombs were visited as holy places where prayers were offered. Once a year the eucharist was celebrated there in their memory on the anniversary of their deaths. The martyr was becoming the ideal believer, making the ultimate sacrifice, for, as Jesus had said, 'Greater love has no-one than this, that he lay down his life for his friends' (John 15:13).

This pattern can be seen in the epistles of Ignatius of Antioch where details about early church doctrine, worship and authority are revealed and the role of the martyr is spoken about. Ignatius was the bishop of Antioch from around AD 69. He was taken to Rome early in the second century under a guard of ten Roman soldiers and was greeted by various Christians along the way. He begged them not to try to intervene with the pagan authorities on his behalf; he desired a martyr's crown and did not want to escape it. Ignatius longed for a martyr's death: 'I am His wheat, ground fine by the lion's teeth to be made purest bread for Christ' (Romans 4).

Here there is boldness and a longing for God, but there is also a reckless abandon that is not seen in the New Testament treatment of martyrdom. A 'rush for martyrdom' developed in the second and third centuries as a form of heroic and deeply committed Christianity.

Polycarp

Polycarp, the aged bishop of Smyrna, was martyred during the reign of Marcus Aurelius, in the mid-second century. He reported to the governor of the province, or proconsul, that he had served Christ eighty-six years, probably having been baptized as an infant. Ignatius reported that Polycarp had known the apostle John and Eusebius suggests that John appointed him as bishop. Polycarp was a strong opponent of groups who sought to Hellenize and distort Christianity, and taught fidelity to the apostles. In an angry mob uprising, he was brought to trial and refused to deny Christ by sacrificing to the emperor. There is a moving account of his death in *The Martyrdom of Polycarp*, a second-century church document, where he is stripped and taken to a pyre and burnt alive. His final prayer is structured like an early eucharistic prayer in which he asks 'that I may be numbered amongst the martyrs, to share the cup of thine Anointed and to rise again unto life everlasting.'

This document is our earliest martyrology or *acta*. The fact that the details are so lovingly recorded shows the great devotion accorded not only to the saintly old man but also to martyrs in general. It also contains the earliest mention of the veneration of relics – the local believers desired to obtain the body so as to have precious relics of the saint – and the earliest mention of the celebration of the eucharist on the anniversary of the saint's death (or 'birthday' into heaven).

Perpetua and Felicitas

In 202 the emperor Septimus Severus forbade conversion to Christianity, ordering that catechumens ('those being instructed') be rounded up and imprisoned. Perpetua and Felicitas (or Felicity) (d. 203) were part of a group of such catechumens. Perpetua, a young mother in her early twenties, had recently given birth to a child and was preparing to be baptized in Carthage. Among her group was a slave couple, Felicitas, who was pregnant, and Revocatus. When Perpetua's family showed concern for her welfare, she replied, '... my prison became a palace to me and I would rather have been there than anywhere else.'

The group were sentenced to death in the arena after their baptisms and a contemporary account of their trials has been preserved in *The Passion of St Perpetua*, possibly edited by the early Christian theologian Tertullian. It contains a series of remarkable visions such as Perpetua entering the arena, being transformed into a man, stripped, and then entering into a contest with an Egyptian (i.e. the devil). She defeated him and stamped on his head.

On the actual day of their martyrdom, a wild heifer was sent out to dispatch the women, which did not succeed. They were executed by a gladiator's sword after much suffering. It seems that Perpetua was in such a state of spiritual ecstasy that she was unaware of much that was happening. It is a striking story with a strong apocalyptic flavour and a definite feminist stance for its day – the martyrdoms of the two women were focused upon much more than those of the several men with them. Moving details are included such as the fact that Felicitas even went out into the arena still lactating as she had recently given birth. Their testimony was long remembered and honoured both in North Africa and further afield.

Christians and the classical world

In the process of Christianity's geographical expansion and the growth of Hellenistic culture, Greek philosophy was embraced by many of the early Christian thinkers who used its terms to articulate the teachings of the gospel. Christian doctrine began taking shape through the philosophical and religious dialogue of those we now call the 'church fathers'.

Justin Martyr

One early example is Justin Martyr (c. 100–65), who works include his *Apologies*. Born of pagan parents in Samaria, he studied philosophy before embracing Christianity around 130. He taught at Ephesus and later moved to Rome and opened a school where he wrote his *First Apology* (c. 155) for the emperor and his sons. His *Second Apology* was for the senate, just after the accession of the emperor Marcus Aurelius, around 161. He also wrote the *Dialogue with Trypho*, probably when in Ephesus (c. 135), engaging Jewish readers. He was martyred around 165 after being denounced as a Christian and refusing to offer sacrifice to the emperor.

Justin Martyr argued that the philosophers such as Plato had known some wise insights from the pre-incarnate Word, or *Logos*, as all wisdom comes from him. It would not have been inappropriate to set up altars remembering their role and honouring the *Logos* at work in them. Here, he was using the common philosophical term *logos*, which in Greek philosophy meant 'reason' or 'word'. In various schools of thought the *logos* could be a rational, enlightening, even divine spark within human beings. In others it was a creative power as well, being used to make the world. How natural it was to link this to the idea of the 'Word of God' in Judaism and early Christianity.

Tertullian

Some rejected Greek philosophy as pagan and a distraction. Tertullian (c. 160–225) wrote, 'Wretched Aristotle!... What does Jerusalem have to do with Athens?' Tertullian was born a pagan in Carthage, received training in literature and rhetoric, and may have practised as a lawyer. He was converted some time before 197 and wrote a large body of apologetic works and moral instructions, mainly in Latin. He was a Scriptural teacher and wrote to defend the Christians against defamatory gossip bandied about Roman society. He wrote his *Apologeticum* (*Defence*) at the turn of the third century, making an impassioned appeal for conversion to Christianity:

> *We are but of yesterday, and we have everything you have –*
> *tenements, forts, towns, exchanges, yes! And camps, tribes,*
> *palace, senate, forum. All we have left you is the temples!* [1]

Tertullian also urged a repudiation of superstition and idolatry, was a moral rigorist and combated heresy. He ended up as a part of the revivalist, end-of-time preaching group the Montanists, named after Montanus of Phrygia in the later half of the second century AD. Montanus's followers believed that a new outpouring of prophecy had come upon them, warning people of the imminent return of Christ, and they looked forward to his literal 1000-year reign. They were strict, rigorous and passionate, and tried to rekindle some of the original fire of early Christianity as they saw it. Gradually, Eastern bishops condemned them as, later, did Rome. Tertullian sided with them, but it is not clear whether he left the mainline church to join them or whether in North Africa they were tolerated more and allowed to operate within the churches. Opposition to them mounted because of their claim to divine inspiration and authority, which they set as equal to that of the apostles and the Scriptures.

Tertullian wrote of the value of martyrdom, declaring that 'the blood of the martyrs is the seed of the Church', and was the first to use the term 'Trinity' in reference to the persons of the Godhead. He articulated the Trinity as 'one substance, three persons' using philosophical terminology (*substantia* and *persona*) up to a point. Tertullian had little time for classical philosophy, devoting more thought to lifestyle and worship in the main. His writings about baptism are an invaluable liturgical source, and his antipathy to infant baptism shows that this practice was not yet established in all Christian communities by the late second century, though it was becoming more widespread.

Hippolytus

Little is known about Hippolytus who was a popular and influential elder, or presbyter, in Rome in the early third century AD. He was a renowned preacher and wrote many texts, covering liturgical matters, Scripture commentaries and works of theology. He wrote a many-volumed *Refutation of All Heresies*, which began by detailing key ideas in pagan philosophy that had laid the foundation for later heresies. He also wrote about the Trinity and developed the idea of the divine *Logos* found in Justin Martyr. For Hippolytus the *Logos* seems to be a divine power, an extension of God's being, which gains personality in the incarnation when he becomes Son. This suggestion of a change in the *Logos* drew much criticism, and Hippolytus fell out of favour for resisting the new pope, Callistus (217–22). [2] During a time of persecution he was exiled to Sardinia where he seems to have been reconciled with Rome.

These men were the apologists, explaining, teaching and defending the Christian faith as they believed it had been handed down from the apostles.

Heresy

We have seen how problems set in once the gospel spread into the Hellenistic world. There are traces of docetism, which could not accept a real incarnation, in the late first century, as can be inferred from the epistles of John, and it was certainly a problem at the start of the second century, as is evident from the writings of Ignatius of Antioch. Ignatius defended the reality of the incarnation against it, and appealed to the eucharist to counter its charge. For Ignatius the bread and wine underwent a mysterious change at their consecration so that they were, in some way, the actual body and blood of Christ. In *Smyrnaeans 7* he wrote:

> ... they will not admit that the Eucharist is the self-same body of our Saviour Jesus Christ which suffered for our sins, and which the Father in His goodness afterwards raised up again...[3]

This is an early belief that the elements contained the real presence of Christ rather than simply symbolizing it.[4]

The Gnostics

Gnosticism was another movement through which Christianity defined itself in this period. The Greek word *gnosis* means 'knowledge', and many Gnostic believers existed in various types in the second and third centuries AD. Some were pagan, some were Christian (and possibly Jewish). It is not clear if Gnosticism was a pre- or post-Christian movement in origin; regardless of this, there are a range of beliefs and mythologies that seem to become more streamlined and predominant by the mid-second century.

Our knowledge of Gnostic belief derives from two sources.

The first is a thorough description of Gnostic beliefs and writings in Irenaeus's *Against the Heresies*. Irenaeus (c. 130–200), bishop of Lyons, was probably brought up in Smyrna, as he had heard Polycarp as a boy, and then became a presbyter at Lyons after studying at Rome. While he was away on a mission to take letters to the pope, severe persecution broke out at Lyons. He returned to find that his bishop had been killed, and he was elected to the see. He wrote about Gnostic groups and defended the orthodox faith in his *Apostolic Tradition*.

There are also fragments and ancient copies of Gnostic texts. A substantial stash of these was found at Nag Hammadi in 1945 in the sands of Egypt. Thirteen codices (early forms of book), written in Coptic, were found preserved in an old crocodile skin. These confirm the accounts given by Irenaeus, showing that he was balanced and fair-minded in his presentation of Gnostic views no matter how vehemently he opposed them. The known Gnostic texts are in the public domain, all translated, including the recently discovered Gospel of Judas, the contents of which Irenaeus had described perfectly.

The origins of Gnosticism are uncertain. Church fathers speculated that Simon Magus was to blame (see Acts 8:18–24) but recent scholarship has detected an eclectic mix of influences drawn from pagan philosophy, the mystery cults and speculative Judaism. Into this matrix the figure of Jesus was introduced and some groups of Gentile Christians came under its sway. They were influenced by teachers such as Valentinus of Rome in the later second century. These groups saw themselves as the spiritual believers, in contrast to the 'soulish' mainline orthodox Christians. They tried to exist within orthodox congregations but were increasingly ostracized and expelled from these as the church fathers argued against them. The Gnostics were adept at reading allegorical meanings into the New Testament that were alien to the original writers. This was the hidden wisdom which they believed the risen Jesus had imparted to the apostles orally.

Proclaiming yourself a 'Christian' no longer meant that you were necessarily an orthodox believer. The Gnostic Christians produced many epistles and gospels, some claiming to be the teaching of New Testament apostles or of Mary Magdalene. It is possible that genuine sections of oral tradition from Jesus or the early church are contained in some of these, but they are, for the most part, a Hellenistic reworking of the gospel, distorting the original beyond all recognition. They contain later, philosophical, mystical ideas and not the original message. They were the product of a process of acute Hellenization with a view of matter as inferior or even evil. The High God was not the creator, and Jesus only appeared to take flesh. He came to awaken souls to their true nature and free them from this world. The basic myths developed as time went on, with many aeons, or levels, and various intermediary angels.

The Gnostic Gospels, composed in the second to third centuries, retold the story and teaching of Jesus in the terms of Gnostic mythology. Some of them make Mary Magdalene a prominent disciple, given special secrets of the kingdom or special *gnosis*. There is never a secret marriage or any suggestion of erotic relationship portrayed. She is more of an ideal disciple. The Magdalene's role also highlights the question of women in early Christianity. Women played an equal role with men in Gnostic circles, taking it in turn to lead worship, celebrate rituals and give counsel.[5]

Marcion and the angry God of the Old Testament

Marcion (d. 160) was a presbyter from Rome who tried to address the question of the morality of God in the Old Testament. He believed that early passages in the Old Testament – such as the slaying of the inhabitants of Jericho, Jael killing Sisera with a tent peg through the head, or stern Torah commandments about stoning – did not sit easily with the ethics of Jesus and the Gospels. Marcion's solution was quite radical. Given the Greek background of the demiurge and the inferior nature of matter, he argued that the creator God of the Old Testament was not the High God and Father of Jesus Christ. He was an inferior. Marcion's Bible thus cut out the Old Testament Scriptures. The New Covenant was totally new, and a graceful revelation of true Wisdom. It was a Hellenistic, philosophical way of making sense of the matter, for which Marcion was condemned as a heretic. The orthodox church knew that it was rooted in the Old Testament and that Jesus was its fulfilment. This was faithful to the apostolic preaching.

Manichaeism

Manes (c. 216–76) was born in the Persian empire. He was a colourful character who began his own teachings in around 240 and was forced into exile in India by the Zoroastrians. He eventually returned to Persia but was condemned by the ruler and executed. Manes took aspects of Christianity (especially writings of Paul) and Gnosticism and developed a highly synthesized mythology with hierarchies and a strict asceticism, including vegetarianism. Satan had stolen the sparks of light from the High God and trapped them in bodies. The prophets, Jesus, Buddha and himself were redeemer figures, seeking to reawaken people to their true identity. Manichaeism had the most developed mythology, cosmology and levels or aeons. Augustine of Hippo (354–430) was a member of this sect for many years before his conversion to Christianity.

Authority

Three ways of understanding authority emerged in the early

church, namely the role of bishops, the rule of faith and the canon of the Scriptures.

Bishops

The bishop became the focus of unity and the successor of the apostles. Ignatius of Antioch had recognized the bishop as the guarantor of orthodoxy. Irenaeus argued that bishops' authority could be traced back to the apostles and that they thus had the correct teachings. This was to counter the Gnostics' claims that they had a secret teaching from the apostles that was only for the initiated. The roots of Irenaeus's claim go back to the practice of appointing elders in the places where the apostles evangelized (see Acts 19:17). The Greek for 'elder' is *presbyter* and later on in the New Testament the term *episcopos* is used, meaning 'overseer'. Were churches originally run by a group of presbyters who later ordained/selected/recognized one of their number as the chief pastor? Or was this pastor set apart from the beginning? These are debates that still run between denominations in Christianity today. However the office originated, by the early second century it had emerged in the form known today and it became a standard of orthodoxy.

Rule of faith

The early church fathers wrote about a 'rule of faith' or the 'apostolic tradition'. This was a clear body of teachings that all orthodox Christians had to adhere to, for example belief in God as creator, and in a proper incarnation and resurrection. They formed the basis of early confessions of faith such as the Apostles' Creed. This was not actually written by the apostles but it summarized their main teaching. It would originally have been used for new converts preparing for baptism. The

creed polemically affirmed everything the Gnostics denied –
God was the creator, Jesus did take flesh and his body rose
from the dead:

I believe in God, the Father Almighty,
the Creator of heaven and earth,
and in Jesus Christ, His only Son, our Lord:
Who was conceived of the Holy Spirit,
born of the Virgin Mary,
suffered under Pontius Pilate,
was crucified, died, and was buried.
He descended into hell.
The third day He arose again from the dead.
He ascended into heaven
and sits at the right hand of God the Father Almighty
whence He shall come to judge the living and the dead.
I believe in the Holy Spirit,
the holy catholic church,
the communion of saints,
the forgiveness of sins,
the resurrection of the body,
and life everlasting.
Amen.

Scriptures

The first Christians used the Old Testament – naturally, as they
were Jews. The Greek translation of the Old Testament, the
Septuagint (or *LXX*), included some books that the Hebrew canon
omitted, such as 1 and 2 Maccabees. (Many of the early Christians
used the Septuagint and the extra books were in use in the Latin
translations until the Reformation, when the Protestants preferred
the Hebrew list.) Gradually, apostolic writings gathered the

same authority. Some of the Gospel sayings were being quoted by the close of the first century as authoritative Scripture. With so many Christian writings around, what was to be included? The ultimate criterion was whether a document was apostolic; this could mean either that it was written by an apostle or that it was composed by someone who knew the apostles and held their correct teaching. The orthodox Christian communities all agreed on the four Gospels and the ten letters of Paul. There were debates about some other books. A Roman list from the mid-second century added 1 and 2 John, James, Jude and Revelation, as well as the Wisdom of Solomon and the Apocalypse of Peter.[6] The early Christian writer Origen (c.185–254) used the following in the third century: the four Gospels, Acts, Paul's letters, 1 Peter, 1 John and Revelation. By the end of the second century the list was fairly well complete with only occasional disputation. The canon was finally fixed, universally rather than by local churches, at the Council of Nicea in AD 325. This was the first general council of the church where all the bishops were able to meet, after years of persecution. It ratified earlier agreement rather than suddenly imposing order and throwing out Gnostic texts. The council simply affirmed what many of the various local, orthodox churches had said before it.

Timeline

c. 37–107	Life of Ignatius of Antioch, who attacked docetism and defended the role of bishops
c. 100–60	Life of Valentinus, who developed a form of highly mythological Gnosticism by the mid-second century in Rome
c. 130–200	Life of Irenaeus of Lyons, who wrote about various heresies, especially the Gnostics

c. 155	Death of Polycarp – earliest account of a martyr
c. 160	Death of Marcion, who argued that the God of the Old Testament was not the father of Jesus Christ
c. 216–76	Life of Manes, who blended Gnosticism and Christianity with aspects of Buddhism and vegetarianism
250–51	Decius's persecution
251–58	Cyprian and Stephen and Novatian disputed about rebaptism of schismatics; Cyprian and Novatus disputed about the lapsed
258	Valerian's persecution

At a glance

- The eucharist began to be celebrated at the tombs of the martyrs on the anniversary of their deaths. Writings about Ignatius, Polycarp and Perpetua and Felicitas show the honour accorded to the martyrs and the desire to embrace martyrdom as ideal discipleship.
- The apologists, including Justin Martyr, Tertullian, Hippolytus and Irenaeus, wrote various defences of Christianity and refuted heresies.
- Terms from Greek philosophy such as *logos* came to the service of orthodoxy and the term Trinity was coined as 'one substance in three persons'.
- Heresies included docetism, denying the physical reality of Jesus; Gnosticism with its varied mythology of redeemer figures, distant High Gods, aeons to ascend through and inner 'knowledge'; Marcion with his rejection of the creator God of the Old Testament; and Manichaeism with its dualistic, esoteric synthesis of various views.
- Authority was defined by appeal to the role of the bishop as

a successor to the apostles; the 'rule of faith' as a body of key teachings and doctrines such as those that formed the outline in the Apostles' Creed; and the canon of the New Testament, largely agreed by the end of the second century.

● Persecutions broke out in the third century as economic decline worsened. Disputes raged through the church on how to treat the lapsed and those who were schismatic, who had broken away to form 'pure' bodies of believers.

Endnotes

1. Tertullian, *A New Eusebius*, ed. J. Stevenson, London: SPCK, 1977, p. 173.

2. The bishop of Rome had begun to exercise a prominent leadership among the early churches as the successor of Peter and the influence of the city as the capital of the Empire. He was often consulted over disputes and his arbitration was sought. Particular views about his universal primacy and authority developed later.

3. M. Staniforth, *Early Christian Writings*, London: Penguin Classics, 1987, p. 102.

4. Similar language and sentiments can be found in the writings of Justin Martyr in the mid-second century; 'For we do not receive them as common bread and common drink; but as Jesus Christ our saviour, having been made flesh by the word of God, had both flesh and blood for our salvation; similarly we have been taught that the food which is blessed by the word of prayer transmitted from him, and by which our flesh and blood are changed and nourished, is the flesh and blood of that Jesus who was made flesh.'

5. Orthodox Christianity allowed women to be honoured as martyrs, and had active laywomen doing charitable work and speaking prophetically. Some were deaconesses, assisting with

the sick and female candidates for baptism. The office of bishop and presbyter, however, was denied to them.

6. Another early favourite was the visionary *Shepherd of Hermas*, a morality tale, with its strict teaching that sin could not be forgiven after baptism. This was an idea that troubled many and made some delay baptism for as long as possible.

3. Constantine, Creeds and Christendom

A look at the design of church buildings in the fourth century reveals a major change. These were now openly and purpose built. Meetings were no longer private and secret, or held in converted houses. Christianity had become tolerated, and had eventually been established as the official faith of the empire. The new church buildings were copies of the style of the basilica in the Roman forum; this was the town hall, the central meeting place where the magistrates would also deliver verdicts. The church buildings each had a central hall, with two side aisles behind porticos. Men would stand on one side and women on the other. Musicians and clergy would be in the centre, and in a semi-circular apse at the east end was a throne for the bishop or the presiding presbyter and seats on a curved bench for the other presbyters. In front of them was the holy table or altar. It was simple and functional, but it was establishing a hierarchy and a new setting for liturgical worship. Behind these developments lay a major change of the heart in one of the emperors of the early fourth century, Constantine. Christianity in the fourth century

AD had to learn to adapt and acclimatize to a time of peace, prosperity and tolerance. It had to learn how to help to wield power. Some reacted by withdrawing into the desert to live holy lives; others vied for influence with emperors and councils as doctrine was debated and refined.

Final days of persecution

After a time of peace for Christianity, when many went about their worship quite openly, persecutions broke out under Diocletian (reigned 284–305). He divided the empire in two and had an Eastern emperor installed, with two deputies to help, called 'Caesars'. An incident in 303 over the failure of a pagan divination, for which Christian onlookers were blamed, led to an outbreak of persecution. The Caesar of the West was lenient; not so in the East where bloody martyrdoms multiplied. This was eventually stopped by the Eastern Caesar, Galerius, when he faced death and asked Christians to pray for him!

The West, however knew its martyrs too. St Alban was martyred at Verulamium in England in around 304. His grave became a place of pilgrimage for many years, marked by a mound of red earth. A fulsome account is given in Bede's eighth-century *Ecclesiastical History*. Alban, a pagan, gave shelter to a fugitive Christian priest. He was moved by the man's holiness and, after some instruction, he converted. The priest was betrayed, but Alban passed himself off as the man, wearing his cloak and presenting himself at the magistrate's court. He was threatened with torture and death unless he sacrificed to the gods, which he refused to do. 'My parents named me Alban,' he answered, 'and I worship and adore the living and true God, who created all things.' His executioner was moved by his witness and refused to behead him. He fell at Alban's feet, begging that he be held worthy to die as a martyr with him.

The tide was about to turn – the faith had become too settled and rooted within the empire. The catalyst was the son of Diocletian's Caesar of the West.

Constantine

Constantine, son of Constantius, Caesar of the West under Diocletian, marched on Rome in 312, having seen a vision of a Chi-Rho[1] in the sun and the message 'In this sign conquer' (*In hoc signo vinces*). The sign was painted on his soldiers' shields and they won against greater forces at the battle at Milvian Bridge in Rome. In thanksgiving he and fellow emperor Licinius proclaimed in the Edict of Milan of 313 that Christians might freely worship. Thereafter, Constantine gradually carried out reforms such as compensating churches for loss of property, abolishing circus games, outlawing crucifixion and ending the practice of facial branding. New, elaborate churches were built and bishops returned from hiding. St Peter's basilica was erected in Rome on the revered and traditional site of Peter's martyrdom and tomb.

The church was free to worship; toleration, rather than establishment, had been proclaimed. Pagan rites still flourished, and Constantine himself worshipped the Unconquered Sun, accepting baptism only on his deathbed from his friend Bishop Eusebius of Caesarea. He could be ruthless, killing opponents and even his own firstborn son. He also took control of the Eastern empire, establishing Constantinople as the New Rome and this served as his headquarters.

The Donatists

During Constantine's reign a man called Donatus led a breakaway group in Carthage, refusing to accept lapsed Christians after the

Edict of Milan and resisting the emperor's lead, which urged forgiveness. Donatus was condemned, appealed without success to a larger group of bishops, and continued to resist. Finally Donatist property was confiscated. The Donatist movement grew numerous in North Africa and had to be allowed to co-exist by the bishops there. Most of North Africa became Donatist.

This controversy over baptism and the lapsed seems peculiar as we see Christian pitted against Christian in a time when the faith was only recently openly tolerated.

Monasticism

Peace reigned for the church at the start of the fourth century after Diocletian. Various men and women reacted against the new, state influenced, tolerated church cult. Anthony (c. 251–356) retreated to the desert of Egypt after giving away his wealth and making sure that his sister was provided for. He spent twenty years as a hermit, undergoing – according to his biographers – three Satanic onslaughts where he was tempted by lewd sights or attacked physically. After this time he emerged from the desert to heal and teach. He was said to be so holy that he wore a hair shirt and was ashamed to be seen eating. A strongly ascetic trait had entered Christianity at this time, whereby the body was to be punished and tamed, if not to be seen as inferior. It is true that Paul had much to say about the struggle of the flesh and the Spirit in his letters, but this had gone further – it was a strict asceticism that seems to have stronger roots in Hellenistic philosophy than in the gospel. Other hermits followed his example and some formed loose communities but lived apart.

After Constantine's conversion people withdrew from society and sought 'white martyrdom' ('red' being laying down your life). They were rigorous ascetics and some of their behaviour sounds very disturbing, even masochistic. There were extremes, but many holy men and women were among them whose counsel and prayer ministry was sought out far and wide. The first monastics were hermits, living firstly alone, and later near to each other so that they could recite prayers together. Larger, more ordered communes were subsquently formed such as that led by Pachomius on the Nile around 325; thousands of people joined this and two separate enclaves for women were established. Basil of Caesarea set out guidelines which have influenced monasticism in the East ever since. Both he and Pachomius sought to curb excess, Pachomius writing that, 'We must refresh ourselves with food and sleep at the proper time even if we don't want to.' Basil urged the communities to engage in charity and educational work. They started hospitals and grew their own food. Peasants could join and find education and a lifestyle that would otherwise have been denied them. There was a close brotherhood and services were a joy for many. Communities could have both men and women, living separately. Some still went too far; Simeon Stylites was expelled as many tried to copy him. He lived on a sixty-foot (eighteen-metre) pillar on a platform for thirty-six years, practising mortifications and hearing prayer requests as well as teaching the crowds.

The Council of Nicea

During Constantine's reign, confusion about the Trinitarian nature of the Christian God came to the fore. Arius, a priest from Alexandria, argued that the Son was not co-eternal with the Father, but rather that the Father was the fount of Godhead and the Son and the Holy Spirit were his creations and thus subordinate. The Son and Spirit were divine and exalted, way above the order of creation, but they were not actually part of God. They were his first creations. He took certain verses as proof texts such as Proverbs 8:22–25:

The Lord brought me forth as the first of his works, before his deeds of old; I was appointed from eternity, from the beginning, before the world began. When there were no oceans, I was given birth, when there were no springs, abounding with water, before the mountains were settled in place, before the hills, I was given birth...

and Colossians 1:15: 'He is the image of the invisible God, the firstborn over all creation.'

For Arius, these taught that Jesus had a beginning; he was not eternal and therefore not divine as the Father was divine. He was a populist and composed songs sung in the market place and at the docks with ditties such as 'The essence of the Father is foreign to the Son.'

Arius was bitterly contested by his bishop, Alexander, and also by the young deacon Athanasius (d. 373), who had already written his work *On the Incarnation*. Athanasius argued that the Son and the Spirit were like rays of light emanating from the Father. They were part of God. Only a saviour who was truly God could save. The corrupted image in humanity could only be restored by God himself descending in the flesh. The creator alone could recreate humanity. He became what we are so we can become what he is, in a sense, by grace. Arius's proof texts were open to other, more orthodox, interpretations. For Athanasius, the belief that the figure of Wisdom was the first of all God's works, having her beginning before the earth was formed, meant that the Son had lived in eternity with the Father. He was eternally begotten (a technical Trinitarian term) of the Father's love; this was an event beyond time and space. Thus, there never was a time when he was not. The use of an eternal begetting is stretched language, trying to describe mysteries. The designation of the Son as 'firstborn' in Colossians 1:15 meant a ruler, one with authority, as a firstborn son was head of the household after his father. It was also a reference to the resurrection – Jesus as the firstborn of the dead, the Risen Lord. It did not say anything about his ultimate origin.

The conflict soared and Constantine called the bishops to Nicea in 325. This was the first general (or ecumenical, meaning 'of the whole world') council of the Christian church. The decisions of such gatherings came to be seen as binding and as guided by the Spirit. The resulting creed spelt out orthodox theology – 'God from God, light from light. True God from true God, begotten not made.' A new term was added, too, that of *homoousios*, 'of the same substance'. This caused ill feeling as it suggested that Jesus was no different from the Father, just another mode of being. (Such a position, modalism, had been denounced as heresy in earlier debates. This depicted the Trinity as one God in three roles, rather like the actor's masks in the theatre. One actor was behind them but he could become three different characters wearing them within the drama.) This was not the intention of the Council of Nicea; its members were trying to say that the Son was fully divine; not created and a distinct divine person.

Arius was ousted and pleaded to be reconciled but he was scapegoated as 'Satan'. Eusebius of Nicomedia was sympathetic but his friend had become a liability. Constantine eventually agreed to reinstate him but the emperor died soon afterwards and this edict was lost to history. The popularity of Arian teaching in the empire showed how new the faith was, and how the Hellenistic world was struggling to understand its terms and dogmas. It was a time of refining, or clarifying. Former pagans could easily believe in a God who had other, lesser deities that helped him, but this was not New Testament, apostolic Christianity. Early views of the Trinity had envisaged a descending hierarchy of Being, rather akin to Neo-Platonism where there was 'the One' (the transcendent High God), the *Logos* (who made the world) and the *Nous* (or 'World-Soul'). It seemed to make sense to most people. God retained his mystery and his emanations did his work, but they were still part and parcel of the Godhead. Arius had pushed the analogy too far, but he would not be the last to stretch the limits.

Christology (the person of Jesus)

Debates over Jesus and the Trinity continued. Constantine's son, Constantius, outlawed the term *homoousios* ('of the same substance') as a novelty and as misleading. More extreme forms of Arianism were being taught and moderate bishops talked about using the word *homoiousios*, or 'of like substance', instead. This was seen as a suitable compromise. They preferred this because it stressed that there were distinct persons and not a form of blurring them together in one lump of divine 'stuff'. The Son and the Spirit were divine and this was somehow part of, or very close to, the Godhead but also different and distinct. Involved in these disputes and maintaining a strictly Nicene orthodoxy, Athanasius was exiled time and again. The next emperor, Julian the Apostate (d. 363), reverted to paganism but lasted only for two years. Later emperors favoured the Arians and exiled the moderate leaders, too. Arianism converted the Goths through a missionary sent by Eusebius of Nicomedia and their numbers swelled the ranks of the Roman army. Disputes took place even while buying and selling bread in the market place, and the games had chariot races run by opposing sides!

Round dances and the Trinity

The Cappadocian fathers, Basil of Caesarea (c. 330–79), Gregory of Nazianus, (328–89) and Gregory of Nyssa (c. 330–95), helped to heal the breach for the moderates and the Nicene party by the time of the Council of Constantinople in 381. They appealed to

Tertullian's model 'one substance, three persons' and developed a more sophisticated Trinitarian theology from that of a hierarchy of being – greatest, greater, great – which had allowed the possibility of Arian views. They saw the Trinity more as a circle, a round dance of being and love where each person lived within the other. This was so-called co-inherence, or *perichoresis*. The Father was the fount, but the emanations of his love were eternally with him and a dynamic inter-relationship ensued from all eternity. The difference between the persons was not of greatness or levels of divinity but of relationship. The Father begets the Son (eternally) and sends the Spirit (eternally). Their motto was 'By the Father, through the Son, fulfilled by the Spirit'.

No human soul?

Apollinarius (c. 310–90), a friend of Athanasius, pushed the orthodox line too far by saying that when the Word became flesh there was no need of a human soul (or mind) in the man Jesus. Human souls are changeable and imperfect, and Christ was filled with the perfect, divine will. This was rejected by all parties and Gregory of Nazianus declared, 'What has not been assumed cannot be redeemed.' Jesus had to be fully human and divine to be saviour. The Council of Constantinople met in 381 and won the day for Nicene orthodoxy, rejecting Apollinarianism and affirming the idea of co-inherence of the persons of the Trinity, as taught by the Cappadocian fathers.

The Nicene Creed that is recited today in churches is based upon that of Nicea and Constantinople but is an elaboration of them. Where the exact text originated from is unknown. The crucial additions to and elaborations of the Apostles' Creed concern the nature of the Son and the divinity of the Spirit:

We believe in one God,
the Father, the Almighty,
maker of heaven and earth,
of all that is, seen and unseen.
We believe in one Lord, Jesus Christ, the only Son of God,
eternally begotten of the Father, God from God, light from light,
true God from true God, begotten, not made, of one Being with
the Father; through him all things were made. For us and for
our salvation he came down from heaven, was incarnate of the
Holy Spirit and the Virgin Mary and was made man. For our
sake he was crucified under Pontius Pilate; he suffered death and
was buried. On the third day he rose again in accordance with
the Scriptures; he ascended into heaven and is seated at the right
hand of the Father. He will come again in glory to judge the
living and the dead, and his kingdom will have no end.

We believe in the Holy Spirit, the Lord, the giver of life, who
proceeds from the Father, who with the Father and the Son is
worshipped and glorified, who has spoken through the prophets.
We believe in one holy catholic and apostolic Church. We
acknowledge one baptism for the forgiveness of sins. We look for
the resurrection of the dead, and the life of the world to come.
Amen.

Establishment, Christendom and the Jews

The fourth century saw the empire tolerate Christianity and then embrace it as the official faith under the emperor Theodosius. He was assisted by Ambrose of Milan (c. 339–97) and paganism was outlawed. Sacrifices were forbidden. Belief was no longer a matter of conscience. Theodosius issued a decree in AD 381 that said of anyone outside the Catholic Church:

The rest, however, whom We adjudge demented and insane,
shall sustain the infamy of heretical dogmas, their meeting
places shall not receive the name of churches, and they shall
be smitten first by divine vengeance, and secondly by the
retribution of Our own initiative... [2]

The Jews were out of place in this new society where only baptized Christians were regarded as proper citizens and attitudes unfortunately became more anti-Semitic. A bishop burned down a synagogue on the Euphrates and Theodosius demanded that he rebuild it. (The Jews had always expected protection under Roman law.) Ambrose stopped the rebuilding, showing a disturbing trait, though he was in other ways a holy bishop and a father-figure to Augustine of Hippo. Jerome even called the synagogues whorehouses and John Chrysostom (c. 347–407), the bishop of Constantinople and an eloquent and inspirational preacher, could say, 'I hate the Jews... most miserable of men...' Jews were to be accused of the horrendous sin of deicide, of killing Christ with tragic consequences in the Middle Ages and beyond. This is a far cry from the teaching of the New Testament, where Paul urged his Gentile converts to honour the Jews for all that had been received from them and believed that they would be saved (see Romans 11).

Augustine's *The City of God*

Augustine of Hippo (354–430) wrote his monumental work when Rome was attacked by barbarians in 410 (the same year that the legions left Britain). Augustine was a convert from Manichaeism, whose Christian mother Monica had tearfully prayed for him over the years. After much heartsearching, he heard a voice telling him 'to take and read', and he read from Romans, hearing the message of the grace of God for the sinner in Christ Jesus. He told this story and that of his intemperate life in his *Confessions*. Many other letters and theological works were to pour from his pen, of which *The City of God* is the longest and most thorough.

Pagans blamed Christianity for the empire's weakness and decline. Augustine argued that the kingdom of God stood forever, whereas human kingdoms came and went. The city of God was not Rome, but the heavenly Jerusalem, Paradise, that was to be established at the return of Christ. He was thinking the unthinkable: a world, a future without the Roman empire. The emperor in Rome was to be no more by the end of the fifth century AD. Augustine had truly read the signs of the times.

Augustine also wrote about the Trinity, using the human analogy of reason, will and understanding as a model for the persons. This began with one thing (pictured as the mind) and examined how it can be three (reason/will/understanding). Others started with the three and went on to see how are they are then one.

It was almost an opposite approach to that of the Cappadocian fathers, with their round dances of love and co-inherence. Some criticize Augustine as being too impersonal. Augustine conceded that all he wrote about such a great mystery was inadequate, but it was better than silence. As Gregory of Nazianus had also admitted, 'To conceive God is difficult, to define him impossible.'

Augustine also spoke of the invisible nature of the true church – who will be saved in the end we cannot see for sure. Some who have the name Christian may fall away, some sinners may repent. The church on earth has to include all the baptized apart from the worst offenders. Whereas membership had been more elitist and strict, it was now more easy and open. In the late Roman empire, you were born into a Christian culture, baptized into it and passed away from it with Christian funeral rites. Augustine was struggling with the problem of establishment and nominalism.

The other areas that exercised his thoughts were those of grace and original sin. He had experienced great grace and knew that he had been a great sinner. These were two strong forces that had to be faced up to in any coherent and orthodox theology. Augustine spoke of election and predestination, where the grace of God claimed and pursued the sinner, whose conversion was known beforehand by God in eternity.

Grace

Pelagius was a Briton and a contemporary of Augustine. Pelagius was trying to revive piety and morality in Rome and he reacted to a reading from Augustine's *Confessions*. Augustine appealed to the grace that helped him live a chaste life after he had failed under his own efforts for so many years. Augustine had written, 'You command chastity. Give what you command, and command what you will.' Pelagius urged self-discipline and God-made laws that should be obeyed with Christ as our example. His exact views are perhaps unknown as none of his writings have survived. His views were condemned by a series of councils, disputing back and forth, though he was also cleared by a synod at Jerusalem and Lydda. Pope Zosimus (410–17) reopened his case and found in his favour at first but it was the church of Carthage that finally stood firm and secured his denunciation. Pelagius seems to have given up the fight and retired gracefully. Nothing more was heard from him and his fate is unknown. It is thought that he may have retired to a monastery in Wales.

Pelagius was understood to be denying the need for saving grace, though his views may have been more subtle than that. Too much talk of 'grace' can lead to laxity. Too much 'law' is a burden and a denial of grace. Orthodox Christianity admits the need for a redeemer, for humanity cannot save itself by its own efforts.

What Pelagius did actually teach is open to debate. It is said that he neglected to speak of original sin and stressed the gift of free-will, the God-given capacity to choose between right and wrong, against sects like the Manichees who saw human beings as spiritually asleep and in slavery to corruption by virtue of being in the body and lost to the light. The transmission of original sin was indeed denied by Rufinus the Syrian, who developed Pelagius's ideas, but perhaps not by Pelagius himself.

East and West and original sin

St Jerome's Latin 'Vulgate' (meaning the Bible translated into the popular, or vulgar, tongue) was produced in the fifth century. This allowed Latin speakers to avoid learning Greek (Augustine hated Greek and struggled with it) and enabled the Bible to reach a much wider readership, since by this time Latin was the established *lingua franca*. Reading the Scriptures in Latin sometimes gave a different sense to that in the original Greek. Augustine's reading of Romans, for example, where Adam is the one 'in whom all men sinned' was more ambiguous in Greek.

The East has never developed the same idea of original sin as the West. All agreed that the first man, Adam, sinned, and that there is an abiding effect of his sin. However, Augustine fashioned a view of original sin that was more akin to original guilt – the guilt of Adam, which is transmitted along the generations. According to this view, we are each guilty of the Fall and live in a state of separation from God.

The church in the East, in contrast, tends to speak of the consequences of Adam's sin as seen in mortality, fear of death and a struggle to do good. One speculation of Augustine's was to hold much influence in the West, though later it was contested and rejected by many. He suggested that the way in which original sin passed down was through concupiscence, that is, the lust that occured between a man and a woman when a child was conceived.

Mary the Theotokos

More disputes about Jesus broke out when Nestorius (d. c. 451), the bishop of Constantinople, rejected increasing veneration of Mary the mother of God and the title 'Theotokos' (literally 'God bearer'). He argued that, 'A creature cannot give birth to the creator, only to a man', and instead posited 'Christotokos' as the correct title for Mary. Since Nicea, and its clear statement of Christ's incarnation and full divinity, devotion to Mary had increased. The mother was honoured because it was her obedience that allowed the saviour to be born, and it was her flesh that the redeemer took. Before this time Mary was honoured as a second Eve by writers such as Irenaeus of Lyons, and a long tradition spoke of her as 'ever virgin', with the brothers of the Lord as step-brothers or cousins.

Bitter disputes ensued with Cyril, Patriarch of Alexandria (d. 444). Powerplays were in force and Nestorius was condemned at the Council of Ephesus in 431. Behind this tension was a difference in emphasis between the schools of Antioch and Alexandria. The former stressed the humanity of Christ, the latter the divinity. Antioch feared that the Alexandrians were teaching a hybrid – a God-man and not God incarnate in a human – and the Alexandrian school was concerned that Antioch was presenting an inspired man (i.e. a man filled by God) rather than a real incarnation. As Cyril said, 'God the Logos did not come into a man, but he "truly" became man, while remaining God.' Or, again, 'Christ was not born as an ordinary man of the holy Virgin and then the Word descended upon him; the Word became flesh in her womb.'

Both sides were using different terms and a different language

– Nestorius used Syriac and Cyril wrote in Greek. Even the
terms used to describe the union of God and man in Christ were
different; when Nestorius spoke of a personal union ('prosopic
union') and Cyril of a substantial union, ('hypostatic union')
they were more or less agreeing but did not realize it because
of their different languages. It sounded as though Nestorius
was watering down the nature of the union, but he was using a
Semitic mind-set where talk of the 'person' was the deepest level
of being you possessed.

Nestorius was condemned for teaching that there was no
real union or incarnation, just that Christ was God filled as an
inspired man, even if the most inspired ever. Were his views
correctly represented? Nestorius is on record as saying that he
would have condemned himself if he really believed what the
Council condemned him for teaching.

Chalcedon

The dispute did not go away. An abbot in Alexandria, Eutyches
(c. 378–454), argued that there was only one being or nature in
Christ, and not two. There was a new being, formed of the union of
divinity and humanity, which others denounced as worship of a
cross-breed. Pope Leo I denounced Eutyches' views as nonsense.
Debate rolled around, and the emperor called a second Council
of Ephesus in 449, which Leo had refused to do, fearing that
Alexandria would manipulate the proceedings. This proved to
be the case, and the emperor supported the Alexandrians' cause.
Leo described it as a 'council of thieves'. After the emperor's
death, a new council was called, which met as the Council of
Chalcedon in 451, but, to his chagrin, Leo was not asked to
preside (though his lengthy, written advice – Leo's *Tome* – was
followed). Chalcedon merely affirmed that Jesus is true God
and true man, with the natures neither separate nor merged

into a hybrid. It set boundaries but gave no new explanations or definitions. In fact, the Alexandrian term, 'hypostatic union' was used and affirmed.

For some this was not acceptable or clear enough and the monophysites (those who believed in a single nature) in Egypt and Syria argued that there was one Christ and not two halves. In fact, the Chalcedonian fathers had never claimed that there were two halves, only that there was a real and sublime union, but that is how some understood them. Differences between Latin and Greek terms did not help. An attempt in 482 by the emperor to make peace was rejected by the pope of the day. The emperor simply asked that adherence to the Nicene Creed should be enough. The monophysite schism over the nature of Christ was the first of its kind between professing, orthodox believers. Only centuries later did dialogue help ease the tensions and move them closer to reconciliation.

Gregory the Great

Gregory was the first monk pope and a great reformer, taking office in 590. He organized relief for the poor, the founding of monasteries, and clergy reform with his influential *Pastoral Care*. He also encouraged missions and developed sacred music with the Gregorian chant.

He was responsible for sending Augustine, a prior, to preach to the Angles and many were baptized with King Ethelbert in 601. The story goes that he had seen English youths in the slave market in Rome. When he enquired where they had come from he said, 'These are not Angles but angels!' Whatever the truth of this, he probably realized that south-eastern England was unevangelized at this time

Gregory's character and views raise questions of church authority. Gregory had great humility and rejected any powerful titles except 'servant of the servants of the Lord'. He rejected the title of Universal Pope (Father) when addressed as such by the bishop of Alexandria. (All senior bishops or patriarchs were known as 'Pope' at one time as father figures for the flock. 'Universal Pope' was a stronger claim, to be the 'pope' of the whole church, East and West.)

The role of the bishop of Rome as successor of Peter and a chief pastor, often called upon to adjudicate matters, was not clearly defined in the early church and this was to cause tensions later as his authority became more clearly defined and heightened with the fall of secular Rome.

Timeline

From 303	Diocletian's persecution
312	Constantine's victory
313	Edict of Milan
Early 4th century	Anthony of Egypt and monasticism
325	Council of Nicea
381	Council of Constantinople
430	Death of Augustine of Hippo
431	Council of Ephesus
451	Council of Chalcedon

At a glance

● Diocletian's persecution began in 303 and Alban of England was one of the well-known martyrs. Persecution ended with Constantine's victory in 312 after the vision of the Chi-Rho symbol. The Edict of Milan brought toleration for Christianity.

- Monasticism began in the Egyptian desert as people sought 'white martyrdom'. After the original hermits such as Anthony came more settled, regulated communities who gardened and engaged in charitable work. The rules of Pachomius and Basil of Caesarea laid the foundations for such a lifestyle.

- Doctrinal disputes over the nature of Christ raged between Arius and Athanasius. Arius demoted the *Logos*/Son to a lesser deity, who had a beginning in time. This resulted in the Council of Nicea and the victory of the orthodoxy viewpoint. Debates continued over *homoousios* ('of the same substance') or *homoiousios* ('of like substance') until the final form of what is known as the Nicene Creed resulted in 381.

- Basil of Caesarea, Gregory of Nazianus and Gregory of Nyssa developed Trinitarian theology with the concept of co-inherence; the persons live within each other.

- Christendom began when Christianity became the only sanctioned faith in the empire under Theodosius, and there were early signs of anti-Semitism against Jewish communities and synagogues.

- Augustine of Hippo wrote in the fifth century and envisaged a world without the Roman empire in his *City of God*. He contributed to the theology of grace and original sin and disputed with Pelagius over the role of grace and works.

- Nestorius of Antioch clashed with Cyril of Alexandria over how to understand the incarnation of the Word, and the role of Mary. Cyril championed the term 'Theotokos' and this won the day at the Council of Ephesus in 431. Later disputes over Christ being one, new, unified nature (the monophysite position) or two natures of God and man continued. The Council of Chalcedon in 451 argued for the language of two natures, causing schism with some Eastern churches.

- Pope Gregory the Great began reforms and sent missionaries to the Angles in the mid-fifth century.

Endnotes

1. The Chi-Rho was an early Christian cross symbol made up of the first two letters of the Greek word for 'Christ'.

2. Bamber Gascoigne, *The Christians*, London: Granada, 1978, p. 35.

4. Monks and Missionaries – The Celtic Church and Beyond

With the fall of the Roman empire in the West in 476 the church found itself in the midst of barbarian invasions. Some of the Germanic tribes were Arian Christians. Christianity survived thanks to the monastic movement and dedicated, fiery missionaries, as well as colonies or areas that continued the faith such as the those on western shores of Britain. The missionary monks carried the faith down through Brittany, into Europe, and out as far as Greenland and Iceland.

Missionary priests or bishops such as Patrick and wandering monks such as Columba converted Ireland and strengthened the ancient Celtic Church in Britain. New converts were won among northern tribes as powerful, prayerful spiritual centres were established, for example at Iona and Lindisfarne. These early monks were ascetic and inspired by the desert fathers from the East, having a close connection with the Coptic Church of Egypt and various Orthodox traditions.

In the Far East, other Christian missionaries laboured, following the silk route as far as China in the first several centuries AD.

These were usually monophysite groups or exiled Nestorians. A creative and flourishing Christian community existed in parts of China until the end of the first millennium.

The Celtic Church

The Celtic Church refers to the churches in northern Gaul, western and northern Britain and Ireland.

Mystical and anti-Roman?

Sometimes popular views of the ancient Celtic Church romanticize the facts. Its adherents are claimed as allies of New Age mysticism and the successors of the Druids, or as virulently anti-papalist. These are gross exaggerations. The first missionaries to Celtic lands, for example Patrick and Ninian in the fourth and fifth centuries, were faithful to the pope, perhaps visited Rome, trained on the continent and held to the same traditions. As time passed and the Saxons arrived, commerce with Rome was cut off or seriously impaired. The Celtic areas were separated and continued in the old ways, ignorant of new developments such as changing the date when Easter was celebrated or styles of clergy dress. When the two sides did meet again there was a clash of cultures and some powerplay. The Celtic stance against missionaries from Rome in the sixth and seventh centuries was not against Rome *per se*, but in opposition to changes that had occurred (some of which seem very small to modern ears). The Latin church was becoming more regimented and organized. The older order of things was more organic and less structured.

Respect for nature and local traditions

What is true in modern popular assessments is that the Celtic

Christians were very close to nature and saw the presence of God there. This is evident in their prayers, poems and blessings:

Deep peace of the running wave to you.
Deep peace of the flowing air to you.
Deep peace of the quiet earth to you.
Deep peace of the shining stars to you.
Deep peace of the Son of peace to you.[1]

Part of a catechism that could date back to Ninian in the fourth century expressed delight that God was reflected in 'every plant and insect, every bird and animal, and every man and woman.' This intimacy with the natural world is similar to that of the early Franciscans years later.

Another feature of the Celtic style was that the missionaries would seek local customs and myths and use them for the gospel, such as the pagan Celtic fascination with the number three, and the threefold natures or aspects of some of the deities. If Patrick ever really did use a three-leafed clover to explain the Trinity, he would have had a ready audience. The structure of Celtic poetry and the idea of charms and runes could be taken up as a way of expressing the gospel. The 'Rune of Hospitality' uses the old custom of showing honour to the traveller:

I saw a stranger yesterday.
I put food in the eating place,
Drink in the drinking place,
Music in the listening place;
And in the sacred name of the Triune God
He blessed myself and my house,
My cattle and my dear ones.
And the lark says often in her song,

Often, often, often,
Goes Christ in the stranger's guise.

Yet these missionaries were like the Old Testament prophets in some ways, too, opposing pagan rituals and temples, tearing them down, felling idols and standing in stark opposition. The example of Patrick lighting his Easter fire is a case in point; he lit the fire of Easter at the same time that the Spring fire was lit by the druids. To dare to light any fire when theirs was lit was to risk death.

The Celtic monks began their work in earnest after the Roman legions had left Britain in 410 and Angles and Saxons were raiding and settling. The ancient British communities shrank into Wales and Cornwall, and some territory along the western coast up to Scotland, as well as an émigré community across the sea in Gaul in the area of Armorica (modern Brittany). For a time warlords rose and fell, protecting the ancient people from the invaders, with names such as Vortigern, Carotocus and Ambrosius. The legends of Arthur found their origin in these times, too. Some areas were settled peacefully by the newcomers and the Britons lived among them. Other places had raids and massacres, with whatever remained of the population displaced. It was a piecemeal, gradual change over the fifth century. The monasteries sought to keep the faith alive and preached to the north and the west, converting Picts and the Irish. There were few contacts with the Saxons or inroads into the Saxon areas. When the Roman Augustine arrived in the sixth century he found widespread paganism in the south and the east of the island.

Eastern influence?

The idea of an Egyptian influence on Celtic Christianity might sound surprising at first, but monasticism had spread from there. Eastern monks travelled to centres in central Europe and

Martin of Tours (d. 397) was instrumental in introducing the monastic life to the Gallic lands in the fourth century. He became a catechumen when still a Roman soldier. He gave half his cloak to a beggar and then had a vision of Christ calling him to the religious life. He worked with Hilary of Poitiers and founded the first monastery in Gaul at Ligugé, later becoming bishop of Tours. These new communities and initiatives needed expert guidance and mentoring, and Egyptian monks travelled to aid them. Similarities are noted between Celtic Christian artwork and Coptic – compare the style of the illustrations in the Book of Kells with Coptic icons, for example, and crosses, emblems and carvings correspond. One inscription reads:

> *House full of delight*
> *Built on the rock*
> *And indeed the true vine*
> *Transplanted from Egypt...*[2]

For the Celtic monks, their deserts were the bogs of Ireland, the craggy isles, rocky hills and the deserted places. The monks sought out places to isolate themselves in their work of prayer, study and worship; these included the beehive stone huts at Skellig Michael eight miles (twelve kilometres) off the Kerry coast, or the lone Gallarus Oratory in the Dingle peninsula. There the members lived off plants and fish, collecting rainwater in cisterns.

To this day Orthodox Christians venerate the Celtic saints as honoured, fellow Orthodox believers from the days of the undivided church.

Peregrinatio

The Celtic monks were wanderers. They did not hide away in a community but travelled, set up a hut, a church, a small monastery and then expected some of the brothers to move on even if they did not do so themselves. This principle of wandering, *peregrinatio*, was not always motivated by evangelism. It could sometimes be evangelistic, as in the case of Patrick or later Aidan in the seventh century who was called from Iona at the bequest of King Oswald to preach to Northumbria. Often, however, *peregrinatio* was about a personal pilgrimage, a penance, a search for silence, peace and God. Along the way, the monk would witness and preach.

Columba, for example, founded the monastery on Iona in the sixth century because he fled Ireland after a dispute over a manuscript. This cost the lives of many soldiers when the local authorities became involved and a riot broke out. In great remorse he vowed to leave his homeland, settling on remote Iona because he could not see the shores of Ireland from there. The result of that voluntary expulsion and settlement was like spiritual dynamite for the north-western Celts, but that was a secondary matter for him.

Peregrinatio can also be seen in the evangelization of Brittany in France. There are specific sites associated with the old Celtic saints, seven men in the sixth and seventh centuries who formed communities, travelled into pagan lands and preached the name of Jesus: Corentin, Patern, Paul-Aurelien, Tugdual, Brieuc, Malo and Samson. From these power-houses of prayer, the gospel spread and pagan Brittany was converted. The episcopal seat was at Dol and this is a pilgrimage and heritage centre to this day.

Celtic missions

The following details are a selection of personalities and events in the mission of the Celtic Church. This is by no means exhaustive, but it conveys the spirit of this people in this period.

Ninian

Ninian was born of noble parents in the Solway Firth region about 360. He went on a pilgrimage to Rome and was made a bishop there. He visited Martin of Tours and founded a monastery (the Candida Casa) at Whithorn, Galloway, in 397, establishing a mission to the Picts. Patrick may have studied with him.

Patrick

Patrick was the son of a deacon and the grandson of a priest. Scholars debate his exact dates, but the consensus seems to place his birth around 390 and his death around 460. Patrick's exploits and details are known through two of his own surviving writings, his *Confessio* and his *Letter to the Soldiers of Coroticus*. The former is his testimony, explaining his sincere calling and missionary work in Ireland at a time when he was called to account for an ancient sin by the bishops in Britannia. (This was something he had done as a youth before his enslavement, which he had confided to a close friend. Was it fornication, theft or murder? We do not know.) The *Letter* was to a warlord in the north of England whose men had raided Ireland and seized some newly baptized believers as slaves, whilst killing others who still had the anointing oil fresh upon them. Patrick was distraught and horrified and he thundered a scriptural sense of judgment across the sea.

The *Confessio* tells the basic story of his enslavement by Irish pirates when he was sixteen, snatched from his birthplace of Bannaventa (location now unknown). His father was the deacon Calpernicus and his Roman name 'Patricus' suggests nobility. Other names are attested in later writings such as 'Sochet' and 'Maewyn'. He would have had Celtic and Latin names.

Patrick worked as a shepherd in the north-western part

of Ireland, a cold and rain-drenched spot. There the nominal Christian was converted and prayed fervently, earning the nickname 'holy boy'. A vision told him to leave and that a ship would be waiting – which indeed it was, 200 miles (320 kilometres) away. After returning home and training (in Auxerre in Gaul or with Ninian in the north) he had a dream about a man called Victoricus calling him to return to Ireland. We do not know who this man was; he could have been a fellow slave. Patrick returned, reaching Armagh by about 433. This became his base of operations and at some point he was consecrated as a bishop. It is not clear if he was sent out at first as a priest or a bishop, for there was already some unsuccessful missionary work in the island, among British settlements along the coast whose inhabitants worked as traders. They had a bishop, Palladius, who seems to have left in failure and exhaustion. Patrick weaves events of his life in with Scripture and shows a fervent reading of the Bible in keeping with the spirituality of his era. He also had visions, holy dreams and felt the fire and presence of the Holy Spirit.

Later works add many other details. Idol smashing, lighting the Easter fire to bait the druids, facing up to the High King of Tara, Loiguire (pronounced like 'Louis'), and preaching about three-leafed clovers are all later tellings. They may be true, but they do not come from his own pen. It was said that Patrick's first convert was the farmer Dichu, who gave his barn for a church; that Patrick confronted his old master, a druid named Miliucc; and that he drove the snakes out of Ireland. Romans had commented years before that Ireland was free of snakes unlike their homeland; however, this pious legend has, of course, the symbolic meaning that he drove out the devil, the ancient serpent.

The poetic prayer 'St Patrick's Breastplate' is named after him though it may not be from his hand. It is riddled with strong,

Trinitarian imagery and a sense of the real power of evil in the world, two things that may have been very much in Patrick's mind as he struggled in pagan Ireland:

> *I bind unto myself today*
> *The strong name of the Trinity.*
> *By invocation of the same,*
> *The Three in One, and One in Three...* [3]

Brigid

Brigid (c. 450–523) was the prioress of a monastery in Kildare, a mixed community of men and women. She was probably baptized by Patrick and as a young woman was determined to take religious vows and live a chaste life. One day her father took her to the king of Leinster, intending to sell her as a slave. When she was waiting in the cart outside, a leper begged for alms. She offered him her father's sword, a fine and expensive piece of craftsmanship. Her father was furious, but the king laughed, seeing that she could never be tamed. He urged her father to allow her to enter religious life. The monastery at Kildare became the largest settlement in Ireland for a time and was known as 'the City of the Poor'. Brigid shares the same name as the goddess of fertility. Legends about the latter have become mixed up with Brigid's memory, with some old rites and offerings to ensure blessings upon cattle transferred to St Brigid.

Columba

Columba was born around 521 and he founded a community on Iona after fleeing Ireland in remorse over the deaths of many soldiers. He had travelled widely in Ireland until he was about forty, setting up monasteries. He was known for his purity of life and his humility. He began to eat simply, taking only nettle soup, which his cook laced with some milk to keep him healthy. Various stories speak of his sanctity and the supernatural gifts, or charisms, of the Spirit that he possessed: Once when staying with a poor farmer, Nesan, for one night, Columba was fed as well as the family could afford. He asked the farmer how many cows he had. 'Five' came the reply. Columba gave his blessing upon the herd and the children of the farmer. He prophesied that he would have 100 cows and it was said to come to pass. With the rich and selfish he could be very different. One such man, Vigen, disdained Columba and refused him hospitality. Columba prophesied thus:

> *The riches of this miser, who has rejected Christ in the pilgrim*
> *visitors, will from henceforth be diminished little by little until*
> *there is nothing. He himself will be a beggar, and his son will run*
> *from house to house with a half-empty bag. A rival will strike him*
> *with an axe and he will die in the trench of the threshing floor.*[4]

Again, these things were said to come to pass.

Columba was also something of a kingmaker, helping with the creation of a new kingdom in Dalraida in western Scotland. He probably introduced sacramental anointing for Christian monarchy into the British Isles.

David

David (c. 500–89) was nicknamed 'waterman', possibly because he was teetotal, or for his habit of standing in water to recite psalms, or as a result of his frequent penitential weeping. He trained at Candida Casa in Whithorn and then returned to Wales, spiritually building on the foundations of the hermit Illtyd, a former druid and warrior who had died in 505.

Aidan

Aidan (580–651) was sent to evangelize Northumbria from Iona. He established a new monastic base at Lindisfarne and trained other leaders such as Hilda, Chad and Cedd. Aidan was a wandering preacher who lived a radical life of simplicity. King Oswald had given him a fine horse but he gave it away to the first beggar he saw.

Cuthbert

Cuthbert (634–87) saw a vision of angels carrying a holy soul to heaven and shortly afterwards heard about Aidan's death. He offered himself for the religious life at Melrose monastery, and continued the work of evangelization in Northumbria. Various miracles are recorded involving nature, such as an eagle dropping a salmon at his feet or sea-otters keeping his feet warm while he prayed in the cold sea.

> *He was in the habit of rising at the dead of night, while everyone else was sleeping, to go out and pray, returning just in time for morning prayers. One night one of the monks watched him creep out, then followed him stealthily to see where he was going and what he was about. Down he went towards the beach beneath the monastery and out into the sea until he was up to his arms and neck in deep water. The splash of the waves accompanied his vigil throughout the dark hours of the night. At daybreak he came out, knelt down on the sand, and prayed. Then two otters bounded out of the water, stretched themselves out before him, warmed his feet with their breath, and tried to dry him on their fur. They finished, received his blessing, and slipped back to their watery home. He was soon home and was in choir at the proper time with the rest of the monks.*[5]

Hilda

Hilda was born in 614 to noble parents. Already baptized, she heard Aidan and embraced the religious life. She became the abbess of Whitby in 657, encouraging the arts, and was patron to the young, uneducated Caedmon. She hosted the Synod of Whitby in 664.

The Gregorian mission

Augustine of Canterbury was sent by Pope Gregory the Great in 596/7 to evangelize the Saxons. The traditional account of Gregory's motivation states that he saw Angle youths for sale in the Roman slave market. Whatever the truth in this tale, it is more likely that the Roman church was aware of a gulf that separated the Saxons from the Celts in the British Isles. The wounds of earlier conquest ran deep and the Celtic monks tended not to wander into their territories. Moreover, the wife of King Ethelbert of Kent was a Christian. This was a point of contact for a new mission to the south. With Ethelbert's support, the monks established their base at Canterbury and proceeded to baptize and preach. Their strategy was to try to convert the rulers if at all possible and to seek their will to enforce baptism on their subjects. Pagan sites were altered and developed into churches rather than being torn down.

After five years in England, Augustine attempted to contact the Celtic bishops. In 602, he asked them to meet him in Canterbury. They refused to travel so long and so far into Saxon territory. Instead they met near Worcestershire, at a spot recorded as 'Augustine's oak'. They debated about the method of baptism, church organization, monastic tonsures (Celtic monks shaved their heads at the front, growing their hair long at the back, after the old druidic practice; Roman monks shaved their heads on the top) and the timing of Easter. The date of Easter was calculated by local traditions in the old, Celtic church and varied across much of Western Europe; Rome, however, had standardized the dating system in 525. The story goes that Augustine called for a sick man to be brought, claiming that the prayers that healed him would show the true, orthodox believer. Augustine won the day. The bishops had to consult their people, meeting again a year later. This time a large contingent also came from Bangor, Wales, having asked a holy man for advice. If Augustine stood to greet them and thus showed them respect, he was a man of God. If not, he was haughty. He did not rise and they took offence. There were raised voices and a curse was put upon the monks from Bangor; years later, thousands were slain in a raid during the battle of Chester.

Matters were not left there. Both sides were to meet much later at the Synod of Whitby in 664, where the Roman party carried the day with their eloquence and their appeal to unity with the pope. Uniformity in dress, government and worship was to follow.

This heated debate shows the strain of separation, misunderstanding, very human suspicion and power play. The ways of Rome had changed since the days of Ninian and Patrick; what was once organic and fluid, with varied local expressions, had become more regimented. Perhaps this was because the last emperor had vacated the imperial throne and the pope now had a responsibility, with his clergy and monks, to hold not only the faith, but the old learning and ways together.

Saxon highlights

Bede (c. 673–735) was at Jarrow monastery where he excelled himself in studies and writing histories and lives of the saints, as well as working on the calculation of the date of Easter following Whitby. His most famous work, *The History of the English Church and People*, records much of our knowledge about the early

history of the British church, Augustine and later events. He told
the story of Caedmon, a young labourer at Whitby who had a gift
for song and composing verse even though he was uneducated.
He claimed inspiration, visions and dreams and turned these
and the Scriptures into Anglo-Saxon verse. We see a wonder at
creation in these that seems to be a continuation of the Celtic
reverence for nature.

Neither did the principle of *peregrinatio* die out after Whitby;
Boniface (680–754), whose real name was Wynfrith of Crediton,
travelled from a monastery in Wessex onto the continent and
evangelized in Germany until he was martyred in Frisia. He was
not afraid to destroy pagan shrines and sacred trees along the
way.

One of Bede's memorable passages contains a parable from
nature in the form of a sermon to King Edwin of Northumbria:

*The present life of man, oh, King, seems to me, in comparison
with that time which is unknown to us, like the swift flight
of a sparrow through the room in which you sit at supper in
winter around the fire while the wind is howling and the snow
is drifting without. It passes swiftly in at one door and out
through another, feeling for the moment the warmth of shelter
of your palace; but it flies from winter to winter and swiftly
escapes from our sight. Even such is our life here, and if anyone
can tell us certainly what lies beyond it, we shall certainly do
wisely to follow his teaching.*[6]

The East

The Celtic monks spread the gospel far to the west in the most
remote areas. Meanwhile, missionaries were taking the gospel
into Persia and along the old silk routes to China. They were
part of the church of the East, which had been based in Syria

under the patriarch of Antioch but Christological disputes and political pressures – mainly over the teachings of Nestorius or later monophysitism – had driven some to separate. Later writers classified the church of the East with its rival patriarch of Antioch as 'Nestorian' and therefore heretical. Marco Polo, for example, designated Eastern Christians he met as 'Nestorian'. Matters, however, were not so simple. Eastern thought was not always so nicely codified and settled. Positions were ambiguous and groups were sent into exile sometimes because of the politics of the day as much as over doctrine. Exiles would also have settled in amongst existing communities of Christians in Persia, which had been growing throughout the times of persecution in the Roman empire. These more ancient groups knew nothing of later, theological disputes.

Thomas

There have, in fact, been eastern missions since the earliest days of Christianity. This is evident from the cluster of traditions about the apostle Thomas as he travelled through Syria and Persia, ending up in India where he is still revered by the Mar Thoma Christians. Oral traditions in South India claim that Thomas came first to the trading port of Cranganore, where he founded his first church in AD 52. He is said to have founded six more along the coast. Cranganore was indeed a trading port, and archaeologists have found copious Greco-Roman artefacts there, especially abundant supplies of Alexandrian coins. He could have travelled there very easily.

The *Acts of Thomas* is a third-century text describing Thomas's preaching and martyrdom. It contains much dubious history but it may reflect some of the truth. For example, it states that Thomas converted King Gundephar of Gandhara; this king did exist at this time. Various traditions are told about his martyrdom, but the simplest is that he was pierced by a lance when involved in a rioting crowd. This was instigated by the Brahmins. Thomas is honoured in a church in Channai where he is thought to have been martyred.

Persia

Christians were in the Persian empire in the early centuries; they followed trade routes and were given hospitality to escape persecution before Constantine. Zoroastrianism, the main faith of the Persians, was a form of monotheism with strong ethics and a belief in a Judgment Day. It was tolerant of Jews and Christians so long as conversions to their faiths did not become excessive. Tatian (c. 110–80) compiled a harmony of the four Gospels, his *Diatessaron*. He was a Persian who studied in Rome and then returned to flee persecution. His document became the mainstay of devotional and liturgical reading in the Persian empire and therefore of Christians who took the gospel further east.

Christians became so numerous in Persia that the Sassasian dynasty which came to power in 226 passed laws to prohibit people from converting from Zoroastrianism. Still, numbers of Christians grew, and it is not inconceivable that Persia would have embraced the gospel as the official faith had it not been for the Muslim conquest in the seventh century AD.

Later excursions of Christians into such areas, after the Christological disputes, were new waves of Christian presence, able to build on what had gone before.

Tibet and China

Missions also went forth to Tibet. The patriarch of the church of the East, Timothy I (727–823) wrote of the need for new bishops for Tibet and describes them as having one of the most significant communities under his care.

The story of the missions to China is a fascinating detective story of discovery. The tale has been uncovered more fully in recent years after the finding of a stash of ancient texts kept hidden in a room cut into the rocks of a remote mountain range. The room was sealed around 1005. There were also artefacts and paintings among the texts dating from the fifth to the eleventh centuries AD. There was material from Buddhism, Confucianism and Taoism, but also Christian material. Jesus is described in oriental terms such as 'the Visitor', 'the Jade-faced One', 'the World-honoured One' and the 'One Sacred Spirit'.

Little was known of the missions to China before the Jesuits came there in 1581. Then, around 1625, a large stone inscribed column, or stele, dating from Tang dynasty (618–906) was unearthed when workmen were digging a grave near Xian. Probably inscribed in 781, it told the story of the arrival of the new religion in 635. On its discovery, a local magistrate saw the similarities with the message brought by the Jesuits. It was now evident that Christians had been established in China centuries earlier.

Reading the old stele, with its text partly in Syriac, and studying the stash of texts, reveals the story. Investigations in the old Christian monastery of Da Quin (meaning 'the West') have also brought to light ancient carvings of figures of Jesus and Mary with distinctly oriental features and symbols.

In 635 a delegation of Christians arrived in Chang-an (now Xian) from Persia. They were formally greeted by the emperor and were led by an abbot, Aluoben. They dressed in white robes and carried icons of Christ. They spoke of the way of Jesus as the religion of Light. The text of the stele reads thus:

The Way does not have a common name and the sacred does not have a common form. Proclaim the teachings everywhere

*for the salvation of the people. Aluoben, the man of great
virtue from the Da Quin empire, came from a far land and
arrived at the capital to present the teachings and images of
his religion. His message is mysterious and wonderful beyond
our understanding. The teachings tell us about the origin of
things and how they were created and nourished. The message
is lucid and clear; the teachings will benefit all; and they shall be
practiced throughout the land.*[7]

The emperor gave his blessing for these Christians to settle and
teach the faith. Monasteries were established, sometimes next to
Taoist ones, and a lively and creative dialogue seems to have
ensued. Later texts reveal a degree of syncretism, but earlier ones
are fully orthodox, setting resurrection against reincarnation, for
example, and using oriental terms for Christian ideas. The saints
became 'the dharma lords', an oriental term for revered teachers
of the Way. By the end of the first millennium the situation had
changed and Christians were no longer welcome. Monasteries
closed and fell into ruin; ancient texts were hidden away. It was
the end of a fascinating, missionary era that began at a time when
the Celtic missions were established in the British Isles and a few
years before the synod of Whitby, as described earlier.

Timeline

397	Ninian opened the Candida Casa monastery at Whithorn
c. 460	Death of Patrick
523	Death of Brigid, founder of Kildare monastery
561	Foundation of Iona monastery
596/7	Augustine's mission to Kent
635	Arrival of Aluoben and his missionaries in Xian, China

651	Death of Aidan, founder of Lindisfarne
657	Hilda became the abbess of Whitby
664	Synod of Whitby
781	Probable date of the Christian stele from the time of the Tang dynasty in China

At a glance

● After the fall of Rome in 476, the work of evangelizing Europe was largely in the hands of wandering, missionary monks. The religious life had been established in the West and was influenced by the desert fathers of Egypt. The old Celtic tribes, and residents of Ireland and Scotland, were evangelized by Celtic monks. They followed the concept of *peregrinatio*, wandering or pilgrimage, wandering from place to place, preaching along the way.

● Ninian evangelized the Picts and Patrick the Irish, Columba founded Iona, David worked in Wales and Aidan was sent to evangelize Northumbria, founding the community at Lindisfarne.

● Augustine's mission was based at Canterbury with the support of King Ethelbert who had married a Christian. Gradually the two sides clashed over various details of liturgy, clerical dress and the date of Easter. Matters were not settled until the Synod of Whitby in the seventh century.

● Bede of Jarrow recorded many details of British church history in his *History of the English Church and People*.

● The church of the East had a rival patriarch of Antioch. These churches were formed from exiled Nestorian and monophysite groups settling with older, more established church communities in Persia. They were vibrant and missionary minded, and reached as far as Tibet and China.

● Persia welcomed Christians escaping persecution and there were numerous believers by the third century. Legend has it that the gospel was first brought there by Thomas, who then travelled to India where he founded several churches.

● A Persian delegation arrived in China in 635 led by Aluoben and was welcomed favourably by the emperor. Christian monasteries were established and flourished until the end of the first millennium.

● The stele telling the story of Aluoben's delegation was unearthed in 1625 when Jesuit missions had started in China.

Endnotes

1. David Adam, *Tides and Seasons*, London: Triangle, 1989.

2. Father Gregory Telepneff, *The Egyptian Desert in the Irish Bogs*, California: Center for Traditionalist Orthodox Studies, 2001, p. 56.

3. *Celebrational Hymnal 24*, trans. Cecil Frances Alexander; Essex: McCrimmons, 1994, Hymn 274.

4. Adomnán of Iona, *Life of St Columba*, trans. Richard Sharpe, London: Penguin Classics, 1995, p. 169.

5. Bede, *The Age of Bede*, (eds.) J. F. Webb, D. H. Farmer, London: Penguin Classics, 1998, p. 58.

6. Bede, *The Ecclesiastical History of the English People*, trans. D. Dumville, D. Farmer, L. Sherley-Price, London: Penguin, 1990, pp. 129–130.

7. Martin Palmer, *The Jesus Sutras*, London: Piatkus, 2001, p. 42.

5. Eastern Orthodoxy and the Great Schism

Constantine had moved his capital to the East, to Byzantium. This was 'the new Rome' with its magnificent buildings and fortifications. Later, with weakening defences in the West, and barbarian invasions, the empire was divided, with two emperors. The Roman empire fell in AD 476 with the deposition of Romulus Augustulus, but the Eastern, Byzantine empire continued until 1453 when the Muslim Ottoman Turks took control and Constantine XI died in the fighting. So for nearly a millennium there was still a Christian empire in the East after the legions had long since vanished in Europe. Its lands gradually diminished with invasions and Muslim advances, but the empire remained until the last emperor fell.

The rise of Islam in the seventh century rocked the social fabric of the Near East and North Africa. The Byzantines were weakened by constant wars with Persia and areas from Syria down along the North African coast were swept into Muslim control. North Africa, which had long been a great centre for Christianity, hosting figures such as Augustine of

Hippo or Tertullian, was transformed. The Christians became a minority.

The churches of the East separated from the West in a series of stages, with the most formal and pivotal stage being that of the Great Schism of 1054. Before this, they had been growing apart for centuries, and attempts to reconcile the two communions failed later on.

Orthodoxy – the church of the seven councils

The word 'orthodox' means 'right belief', and is derived from the Greek words *orthos* (right) and *doxa* (belief). The Orthodox churches believe that they have preserved primitive Christian belief and customs intact, whereas other churches have only partially handed these on. A great emphasis is laid upon tradition, *paradosis*, meaning 'that which is handed on'. This is the apostolic faith with its full teachings and blessings. The Eastern churches came to see themselves as more faithful to apostolic teaching than the Latin West.

The Orthodox Church's faith is based upon the seven ecumenical councils as well as the faith of the apostles and the Scriptures.

325	Nicea
381	Constantinople
431	Ephesus
451	Chalcedon
553	Constantinople
680–81	Constantinople
787	Nicea

The first four of these councils were covered in the previous chapter. The fifth worked on the nature of the union of the divine/human in Christ, rejecting the monophysite position. A number of churches in the East left the Orthodox communion after Chalcedon as they feared that a true union of God and man in Christ was not being affirmed – these became known as the Oriental Orthodox churches and included the Copts, the Ethiopians, the Armenians and some Syrian churches. These believers are monophysites, believing in one nature, the God-man. Early attempts at dialogue proved fruitless, partly because of politics and the separations after the rise of Islam, and partly because of different language and misunderstandings. The sixth council condemned monothelitism (the belief that there was only one will, namely God's, in Christ) thus making him less than fully human. The seventh council defended the use of holy icons against the iconoclasts. During this period church decorations and icons had been removed and destroyed, amidst fears that these encouraged idolatry.

Church decoration had been minimal at first. Christian symbols and paintings of biblical scenes adorned graves and meeting places in the catacombs, the Roman underground cemeteries. The scenes were often of bread and fish, Jonah and the whale (suggesting resurrection) and the good shepherd. Gradually, after Constantine's conversion, new church buildings included some symbols and images in similar fashion; for example, in the East some churches had a painting of Jesus on the curtain separating the sanctuary area. The style was realistic in the early days, following that of funeral portraits that have survived the ages and can be contrasted and compared. Icons painted on wood that could be transferred from place to place were also realistic at first. One of the oldest surviving examples is of Christ from the sixth century in St Catherine's monastery in Sinai and there are five from this period of the Virgin and Child extant in and around Rome. These are real faces, with proportional limbs. Later icon painting was far more stylized, following elaborate rules – visual codes rather than portraits.

The change came after the iconoclastic controversy in the eighth century. Emperors such as Leo III in 730 banned the use of icons and ordered that they should be destroyed. John of Damascus (c. 675–749) agued that they were not idols, for when God took flesh, aspects of the creation could house the creator, and his invisible image could be seen through them:

> *But now that God has appeared in the flesh and lived among men, I make an image of the God who can be seen. I do not worship matter but I worship the Creator of matter, who for my sake became material and deigned to dwell in matter, who through matter effected my salvation...*[1]

His arguments helped to win the day against the iconoclasts. Image and incarnation are closely aligned, as Jesus is indeed, for Christians, the human face of God. Since the seventh ecumenical council and the restoration of images, icons have become a beloved and integral part of Eastern church worship and spirituality, with prayers and devotions offered before them. There is a series of types of portrait of Christ, Mary and the saints with established symbolism at play. Icons of Christ are a symbol of what believers really worship; as Basil of Caesarea put it, 'The honour given to the image is to the prototype.' The saints point beyond themselves to the glory of God who indwells and transfigures them.

Patriarchs and churches

The seven councils established the rule of the pentarchy – the five patriarchs of Rome, Constantinople, Alexandria, Antioch and Jerusalem. (Later patriarchates were to be established, such as Moscow as this realm was free from Muslim control. After the fall of Constantinople in 1453, Moscow was seen as the third Rome and the ruler adopted the title 'Caesar' ('Czar').)

Eastern Orthodox churches became self-governing, having *autocephalos* status. They are in communion with the others, and linked to a patriarch, but can decide certain matters on their own and form an independent body. A patriarch is a senior bishop and not the same as the Latin pope. The Orthodox do not have a pope figure, in the sense of a universal bishop, but the bishop of Rome was also respected as a senior bishop in the early church, the 'first among equals'. Claims to overall authority were rejected and this was an ongoing source of tension between the East and West.

Conversion of Russia

Patriarch Photius of Constantinople (c. 810–95) sent two brothers from Thessalonica; Constantine (known as Cyril when he became a monk) and Methodius to preach to the Slavic people around the empire. They began an enormous work of translation putting liturgies and the Bible into the Macedonian Slavic dialect in which they had become fluent around the ports of their childhood. Their real work began in AD 863 when they went to Moravia. They met resistance from German missionaries who were trying to impose Latin rites (Orthodoxy has always tried to deliver a liturgy in the vernacular of the people). Cyril appealed directly to the pope and was given an audience. He was granted permission for a Slavonic liturgy but the Germans would not stop harassing the Eastern missionaries and eventually, after their deaths, Latin rites held sway. The missionaries' work, however, spread to the Bulgarians, who accepted the jurisdiction of Constantinople. From there, the gospel entered Russia. The story goes that Vladimir, Grand Prince of Kiev and all Russia, sent envoys to report on the different religions. They saw Latin rite worship in Germany but were unimpressed. Islam was rejected when Vladimir heard about the ban on alcohol. Their visit to Constantinople brought the following report:

> *The Greeks led us to the edifices where they worship their God and we knew not whether we were in heaven or on earth. For on earth there is no such splendour or such beauty, and we are at a loss how to describe it.*[2]

Filioque

One doctrinal difference between East and West arose from the West's addition of a clause, *filioque* (Latin for 'and the Son'), to the Nicene Creed. This then read, 'the Holy Spirit who proceeds from the Father and the Son', teaching a double procession of the Spirit from the first two persons of the Trinity.

This began as a speculation in the West with Augustine of Hippo where the Spirit was the facilitator of the relationship between the other two persons, a kind of divine go-between. It gained acceptance and was inserted in the creed in parts of Europe, becoming standard by the end of the first millennium. The Eastern church never followed suit. It feared that this confused the persons and ran the risk of making the Spirit less personal. He became a relationship and not a person in his own right. The East also objected to the unilateral insertion of a new phrase in the creed; if the creed was the result of a general council of the whole church, then no one part of it was authorized to make an addition.

In John 15:26 Jesus says he will *send* the Spirit who *proceeds* from the Father. Sending and procession were seen to be different. The Eastern churches have sometimes spoken of an eternal procession from the Father and a temporal mission, or sending, from the Son. Thus, in the history of salvation, *on earth*, the Son sends the Spirit.

Augustine did not exactly claim that the Spirit proceeded from the Son in the same way as from the Father. The former was *per donum Patris*, 'through the gift of the Father' and the procession from the Father was the principal one, the source. Such subtleties of expression and difference in language can, and did, cause great misunderstanding.

The Great Schism

Clearly tensions had been mounting between East and West for some time. The *filioque* debate illustrates this as well as the problems that Cyril and Methodius encountered over Slavic liturgy. There were other differences in liturgical detail too. For instance, in the East the ceremony of anointing with chrism oil (confirmation) was held at the same time as baptism, whereas in the West there was a delay between the two. The Western practice enabled the young candidate to be presented to the bishop as soon as possible after the baptism by the local priest. In the East, the bishops delegated the task of anointing with holy oil to their clergy.

Similarly, by the turn of the first millennium, Latin rite priests were celibate but some could still be married in the East. The Council of Nicea had established an earlier rule that the East continued to follow. A married man might be ordained a priest, but a single one remained celibate and became a monk. Latin rite clergy were clean-shaven, too, and unleavened bread was used in their eucharists.

These were secondary matters; the greatest problem was that of the authority and role of the papacy. While the Orthodox affirmed and respected the pope in Rome as a senior bishop to whom they would readily turn for advice to settle disputes, the

West saw the pope as claiming a universal jurisdiction beyond his role as patriarch of the Western church. The first schism between East and West happened in the ninth century, briefly, when Pope Nicholas I opposed the appointment of Photius as patriarch of Constantinople in favour of the deposed Ignatius. The pope reprimanded the emperor, Michael III. This was eventually ended by a council presided over by Photius in AD 879. A difficulty between pope and patriarch at that time would not have been taken as a sign of real and abiding disunity between East and West; that was still unthinkable. It was a temporary affair.

Things came to a head in 1054 when Patriarch Michael I Keroularios closed Latin rite churches in Constantinople. Papal legates were sent and were treated appallingly by the patriarch, despite attempts by the emperor to make peace. On 16 July Cardinal Humbert placed a bull of excommunication on the altar of the church of Hagia Sophia in Constantinople. The patriarch declared formal condemnations, known as anathemas, on those who had composed the bull. This was a personal spat, and the mutual condemnations were only meant to be personal, and were not meant to affect the whole of the Eastern and Western churches. Nevertheless, the effects of this local dispute took on far reaching consequences and led to the breakdown of communion between East and West. Despite attempts at formulas of reunion in church councils, no lasting agreement was found. Matters were worsened by the sack of Constantinople during the fourth crusade in 1204 when crusaders sacked Constantinople and butchered many Eastern rite believers; indeed Orthodox Christians trace the real breakdown to 1204.

Easter

Another source of tension was how to calculate the date of Easter. Easter is the feast of feasts in Eastern Orthodoxy, standing in a class of its own with twelve other great feasts around it in the Christian year. Controversies frequently surrounded the method of dating the festival. The Jews used a fixed date, 14 Nisan, to set the date of the Passover. Christians sought to secure the first Sunday after this, but rival methods set this at different times. Alexandria always set it after the vernal equinox, whilst the church at Antioch followed the Jewish reckoning. Nicea adopted the Alexandrian system universally. However, later differences emerged between the Roman calculations and the Alexandrian, which could lead to various regional differences. St Augustine noted that in 387 Easter was 21 March in Gaul, 18 April in Italy and 25 April in Alexandria. Rome finally came into line with Alexandria in 525.

This common dating and usage survived the Great Schism but years later debates took place over whether to follow the older Julian calendar or the newer Gregorian calendar. Today, some Orthodox follow one calendar, some another. This means, for example, that Christmas for some Orthodox is 25 December, but for others it is 7 January. To complicate matters further, virtually all Orthodox believers celebrate Easter according to the Old Style (i.e. the Julian calendar). This means that Orthodox Easter varies from the Western one, only occasionally coinciding.

Sacraments

The Eastern churches did not develop the same sacramental theology and system as the Latin West. This was another point of departure, though not as serious as questions of authority or Trinitarian theology. There are seven sacraments that are acknowledged, as in the West – baptism, chrismation (confirmation), eucharist, confession, marriage, holy orders and anointing of the sick. However, many other actions are 'sacramental', too, such as the rite of monastic vows, the blessing of water at Epiphany, and the veneration of holy icons. Icons are best understood in Eastern theology as sacramental objects, conveying the blessing of the presence of God, Christ or the saints as 'windows into heaven'. There was not the same definition and codification as in the Latin West when sacramental theology was developing.

A charismatic church

There is a strong sense of the invocation of the Spirit in the Orthodox churches. Alongside the rituals and liturgy, there has always been a strong sense of spiritual presence; personal experience is expected and encouraged as a norm. The gifts of the Spirit have never died out, though they are not common. There is a tradition of the holy elder – a layman, monk or priest who is so blessed that people come to him for prayer counselling. In the Russian church, the elder is the *starets*, and these men have a rich tradition of inspired individuals with gifts of knowledge, wisdom and healing. Some teachers have urged people to undergo a personal baptism of the Holy Spirit; some, such as St Symeon the New Theologian (AD 949–1022), have also spoken of a gift of tears which can come upon one when the Spirit is felt.

In this way the Eastern churches have kept a strong link with the more open, and more spontaneous, charisms of the early Christians despite the role of tradition and liturgical structure.

The Jesus Prayer

Orthodox spirituality benefits from the tradition of using short, repeated prayers as a way of devotion, intercession and meditation.

The desert fathers (the monks) used simple prayers and chants, taken from Scripture or using the name of Jesus, to aid them in their meditation. They tried techniques of repetitive prayer or chanting to centre their minds and still themselves, speaking of the 'prayer of the heart'. A rich tradition of prayer and devotion thus grew up separately from Western forms. This is a reminder how far monasticism laid foundations for Eastern spirituality.

Orthodoxy has always taught that the mind must dwell in the heart when praying. Believers need to seek an inner silence from their own anxieties, works and words so that they can actually listen to God within by the Holy Spirit. Some profound teaching on prayer states, 'Why speak at length? Prayer is God, who works all things in all men' (St Gregory of Sinai, d. 1346). There are no rules for how to pray, and many tools are on offer. One popular one in Orthodoxy is the use of the Jesus Prayer, a use of the name of Jesus which developed from the earlier devotions of the monks. This has taken various forms:

Lord Jesus Christ, Son of the living God, have mercy on me, a sinner
Lord Jesus Christ, Son of God, have mercy on me, a sinner
Lord Jesus Christ, Son of God, have mercy on me
Lord Jesus, have mercy on me
Jesus, have mercy on me.

This can be repeated over and over again, silently, or aloud. It can be accompanied by breathing techniques. Though some people seek to say a certain number of these per day, the usual advice is to forget how many are recited, but to enter the spirit of what is being said. A knotted prayer rope has developed as an aid to concentration.

The liturgy

John Chrysostom (c. 347–407) adapted and shortened the Liturgy of St Basil that was in use in Constantinople. There were many different local liturgies in use at the time, and that of St John Chrysostom became popular and the standard in the East. To this day the Orthodox use this liturgy as the norm, with that of St Basil used ten times per year, and that of St James once a year. A common, basic structure can be discerned akin to that in Western rites, but there are other traditions, litanies, repeated prayers, rituals and chants. The liturgy was divided into these main parts:

● The preparation of the bread and wine.
● The Word, with litanies, psalms, chants and readings. The Little Entrance has the bringing of the Gospel book out among the people for the reading.
● The Eucharist, with the Great Entrance where the elements of bread and wine are brought to the holy table, the peace, the creed, the eucharistic prayer and litanies, the communion and final blessing. Communion is received on a spoon as the bread is mixed with the wine. The bread is leavened and cut into small cubes.

Orthodox liturgy used repeated verses and chants as well as short and long litanies of supplication as various things were prayed for again and again throughout the service. Orthodox churches developed screens separating the sanctuary area from the people. A separation of the sanctuary and the altar from the body of the church also developed in the West. There the rood screen was adored by an image of the crucified Christ with Mary and St John usually in attendance. This had some decorated panels but many open spaces or grilles. In the East, the screen became more filled in with doors and thick curtains obscuring all view of what lay behind. This was the iconostasis, where rows of icons came to be depicted. There were doors set into this. Through the central or 'royal' doors the Gospel book was brought out to be proclaimed. Later, at the offertory, the gifts of bread and wine were taken through them. The doors were then closed for the consecration and the priest and deacons brought the blessed elements out for communion. This created a sense of mystery and echoed the Old Testament tabernacle. The throwing open of the doors symbolized heaven coming to earth and grace coming among the people through Christ. A sense of the sacred space of the sanctuary, and the need to approach this with reverence, grew universally in the early centuries of the undivided church, though the separation of this sacred space was more acutely presented in the East.

Timeline

4th–8th centuries	The seven ecumenical councils
8th century	The iconoclastic controversy
861–79	Photian schism
1054	Great Schism between East and West
1453	The fall of Constantinople (Byzantium)

At a glance

- The empire was divided between two emperors, the Western empire falling in 476 and the Eastern lasting until 1453. The North African church fell into decline because of the rise of Islam.
- The Eastern churches recognized seven councils, including some that took further stances against the monophysites and

the heresy that there was only one will (divine) in Christ. The final council dealt with the validity of images.

● The holy icon in the East gradually developed from a form of realistic decoration to stylized objects of devotion that were sacramental as 'windows into heaven'.

● The Slavs were converted by the missions began by Cyril and Methodius in the ninth century.

● Controversy raged over the insertion of the *filioque* ('and from the Son') clause in the creed by the end of the first millennium. This seemed to teach a double procession of the Holy Spirit.

● A temporary schism happened in the ninth century over the pope's rejection of Patriach Photius but this was healed. The Great Schism of 1054 followed the falling out of the papal legate and the patriarch of Constantinople and despite various attempts, this never healed. Matters were made worse during the crusades when Constantinople was sacked and sometimes Orthodox Christians were massacred by Western militia.

● Minor disagreements existed over the role of married clergy, the use of leavened bread, the date of Easter and how sacraments were defined. A major disagreement was over the authority of the pope.

● A rich spiritual tradition developed in the East from the desert monks, using short, repeated prayers such as the Jesus Prayer, and a belief in the continued existence of gifts of the Spirit, or charisms, with holy elders sought out for prayer counsel.

● The liturgy of the eucharist was formalized in the fourth century by John Chrysostom with a different tradition of symbolism, chants and litanies than that of the West. The separation of the sanctuary from the body of the church became more marked in the Eastern churches than in the Western churches.

Endnotes

1. John of Damascus, on Icons 1 and 16, quoted in Timothy Ware, *The Orthodox Church*, London: Pelican, 1963, pp. 131–32.
2. Bamber Gascoigne, *The Christians*, London: Granada, 1978, p. 48.

6. The Medieval Church

The Middle Ages included many epochs and much social change. Studying the medieval church covers several centuries including the renaissance, the great rebirth of classical learning. For our purposes, the medieval period will cover the vast stretch of centuries from the rise of Islam in the seventh century to the start of the sixteenth century and the eve of the Reformation. In this period, Europe began to settle down into a network of kingdoms and fiefdoms, with a revival of Roman law to a degree, exercised by the central office of the papacy. An attempt to recreate the empire in the West occurred with the role of the Holy Roman Emperor from the ninth century onwards; crusades were sent to the Holy Land; attempts at reunion with the Eastern churches failed and Constantinople fell to the Ottoman Turks. Beyond this, increasing literacy brought new lay movements and some demands for reform.

Life in the church

Medieval Europe had one church, the Catholic Church, headed by the pope in Rome. There were some Jews in large cities, who were periodically persecuted and had their movements restricted, but everyone else was a Catholic Christian. People were born into the Catholic Church, were baptized, married, and died in it with a requiem mass. There was no room for unbelief or scepticism unless it was well hidden in jest or philosophical speculation, and then great care had to be taken. There were, however, Christian splinter groups who were branded as heretics such as the Lollards, the followers of Wyclif (c. 1330–84). There were the great festivals of the church such as Christmas and Easter and a host of lesser celebrations on saints' days. These were the 'holy days', from whence we derive 'holiday', and the average medieval citizen would rejoice in their gaiety and the time off from labour. There were many holy days celebrating various international and local saints.

Church was compulsory on Sundays and the mass was in Latin. The power of the pen and the book was in the hands of the clergy (in fact, the term 'clerk' comes from 'cleric' for monks wrote legal texts and drew up contracts). Their power, and the power of the church, was immense, and where there is great power, there will be corruption and self-serving. Stories abound of semi-literate priests who knew little Latin and mumbled the mass, of corpulent and profligate monks, or bishops who might often be absent from their sees, as well as popes who wined and dined and kept mistresses. We can catch a sense of the medieval wit and satire that was scathingly pointed at religious figures who lived worldly and bawdy lives, far below their vows, in some of the nuns, monks and clergy in Chaucer's *The Canterbury Tales* (c. 1387).

People were not anti-religious, just against hypocrisy and injustice. Many priests were faithful pastors and taught their flock. The monasteries were places of healing and charity, forming the foundation of the great hospitals such as St Bartholomew's in London. The rhythms and patterns of the medieval church generally satisfied the populace as can be seen in the work of historians who have searched through inscriptions and wills, old documents and churchyards to find a vibrancy about medieval Catholicism in the popular sphere. People generally found help and solace in the faith and believed in it. There was rhythm and celebration throughout the seasons and the life cycle; there was corruption, there were movements for reform, but there was holiness and satisfaction with much of the status quo.

The Bible, teaching and popular devotions

For many years, because the Bible was in Latin, lay Bible studies were impossible for all but a few educated folk. Then came the rise of the educated merchant classes who had the aid of manuals and primers, encouraged by the invention of printing in the late fifteenth century. Worshippers sometimes relied on personal teaching by faithful priests. Having the services in Latin clouded meaning for some now that it was no longer a living language, though people should have been taught the basics of the services and would know what was going on. The medieval mass had a sense of sacred, reverential awe as the people said their rosaries and other prayers, stopping to adore the newly consecrated bread and wine with the priest. How much Bible or basic doctrine ordinary people knew until the rise of greater literacy depended upon their pastors and upon various popular devotions, festivals and their stories, mystery plays and the imagery found in churches.

Local churches would have been ablaze with colour. Fading wall paintings that depict scenes from the nativity and the passion, as well as various saints' lives, can be seen in ancient parish churches in Europe; then they were strong, clear and vibrant. There would have been floral and abstract patterns, too, all in vivid colours. It was like worshipping inside a bold comic strip, and this told the stories to those who could not read.

Devotions such as the rosary put something into the hands of the laity. This started as a lay psalter, a set of 150 meditations and prayers that corresponded with the 150 psalms that were recited through the daily services of the monks. It took lay people through many stories from the Gospels, setting these firmly in the mind and helping people to learn the gist of them by heart. The Joyful Mysteries told the story of the birth; the Sorrowful Mysteries told the story of the Passion; the Glorious Mysteries, the resurrection, ascension and Pentecost. The idea was to meditate on a story and then recite a set of prayers to dwell on the wonder of the incarnation. These prayers have grown and developed over the ages and the Eastern churches have different forms. In the medieval Latin church they were originally 'Hail Mary, full of grace, the Lord is with thee. Blessed art thou among women and blessed is the fruit of thy womb, Jesus.' A petition for the Virgin's intercession was added later, 'Holy Mary, Mother of God, pray for us sinners now and at the hour of our death.' The 'Hail Mary' conflates two sayings from the Gospel of Luke – one from Gabriel and one from Elizabeth (Luke 1:28; 42). The 'hail' in the prayer implies not worship but greeting. 'Hail', *avē* in Latin, means 'Greetings', and the prayer is based upon Gabriel's greeting.

Latin was the language of the educated and of the realm. It was international, and allowed friends and merchants, prelates and princes, to converse across Europe. The Englishman Sir Thomas More and the Dutchman Erasmus, for example, were good friends and conversed and corresponded in Latin, though they knew not a word of each other's own language. Latin was not the vernacular, but it provided international possibilities.

In an age where the educated wrote and conversed in Latin, the church authorities feared to allow the less educated to have access to the Bible in the vernacular as this might give rise to many misunderstandings and private interpretations. Even without such access, there were heretical movements which distorted and confused aspects of church teaching.

Going to a shrine

Shrines did their work in teaching and attracting the ordinary people as well as the learned. Pilgrimages were levelling experiences, whether they were to the shrine of the martyred Thomas à Becket at Canterbury, to Rome itself with the tombs of Peter and Paul, to Santiago de Compostella in Spain or to Walsingham in Norfolk, and something of the pleasure, pain and camaraderie of the journey can be seen in Chaucer's *The Canterbury Tales*. Compostella gave rise to the wearing of the scallop shell as a sign of being a pilgrim, a shell that signified St James, whose relics were said to be there. Going on pilgrimage could be an international affair, encouraging travel across the continent.

The Walsingham shrine began when, in 1061, the Lady Richeldis claimed to have had a vision of the Virgin holding the Christ child, who implored her to build a copy of the house in Nazareth where the holy family lived. The route to the Holy Land was barred at the time owing to the rise of Islam. Pilgrims flocked to Walsingham from all over Europe, and it became known as 'England's Nazareth'. There was a holy well, and people claimed all sorts of cures. A large friary was built up around the shrine and the monks drew in great wealth as they operated this medieval attraction. Pilgrims removed their shoes at the nearby Slipper Chapel and walked the mile to the Holy House. Monarchs came as pilgrims, too, including Henry VIII, who eventually closed it along with all other religious houses.

Schoolmen

The universities of Europe arose gradually from groups of scholar clerics around cathedrals. In most of Europe the scholars formed guilds to protect their rights in a town or to discipline wayward students; in Italy the students themselves formed the guilds. The term for the guild was *universitas*. The first universities to rise were at Oxford, Cambridge, Paris, Bologna, Montpelier, Padua, Salamanca and Toulouse. They taught the seven liberal arts, a Greco-Roman body of knowledge. These included the trivium ('three ways') of grammar, logic and rhetoric, and the quadrivium ('four ways') of arithmetic, geometry, astronomy and music. Philosophy and logic were also taught to undergraduates. Graduate schools taught medicine, law and theology. The scholars were known as the Schoolmen or the Scholastics and their writings gained precedence in the intellectual world of the time. They were concerned with systematizing, codifying and speculating. The world was made by a rational creator and thus could be understood and all knowledge needed to be gathered under Christian oversight and insight. A great impetus came from the rebirth of learning during the renaissance as ancient manuscripts, largely written in Greek, were rediscovered. The monasteries had preserved many ancient texts from the classical world, but others had been lost or forgotten. The rise of Islam resulted in their discovery via Muslim scholars who translated them from Greek into Arabic. Traders and soldiers discovered them and brought them back to the West. Particular attention was given to Aristotle, whose works were made known through the Muslims of Spain, Italy and North Africa.

Platonism had been the intellectual undergirding of medieval thought until this time, with its philosophy of eternal ideas or forms of things in the mind of God (for example, a particular chair was an imperfect reflection of God's eternal idea of chairness).

Aristotle did not follow Plato. He sought to examine things in themselves and saw a purpose (*telos*) for each thing in the world without recourse to higher realms of Ideas or God. This had a revolutionary effect upon the medieval scholars.

Aristotle had room for God as the 'unmoved mover' who was separate from his creation and cared nothing for it. The Schoolmen used insights from Aristotle but Christianized his thought. To do this they had to have a definite divide between faith and reason, or revelation and reason. There was much about the world that could be known by observation and human logic. There was that which could not be observed and measured, the spiritual or eternal dimension. This was known through revelation in the conscience, through the Scriptures and teachings of the church. The three great Schoolmen were Bonaventure (1217–74), Albert the Great (1200–80) and Thomas Aquinas (1225–74). Bonaventure was the mystic, Albert rediscovered the thought of Aristotle and Aquinas used this in his *Summa Theologica*.

Thomas Aquinas, known as the 'Doctor Angelicus', was the youngest son of Count Landulf of Aquino, who sent Thomas to the Benedictine school at Monte Cassino. He finished his liberal arts course in Naples in 1240 and developed a belief in an intellectual calling. He sought to join the Dominican friars but his parents refused and even imprisoned him for several months to weaken his resolve. They failed, and finally relented. He joined the Dominicans in 1244 and studied in Paris from 1245–48 where he discovered Aristotle. He taught in various other places, returning to Paris in 1252 and gaining his Master of Theology in 1256. After lecturing in Italy, he was back in Paris in 1269 and then moved to Naples in 1272 to set up a new Dominican school where he wrote his magnum opus, the *Summa Theologica*. This was a vast collection of treatises, questions and articles in three parts. The first part (*Prima*) deals with the nature of God and creation; the second (*Secunda*) with God's relationship with humanity; and the third (*Tertia*) with Christ as the way to God. *Tertia* covered material on the sacraments and was not completed in his lifetime, being finished from his notes and commentaries. He died at a Cistercian monastery in 1274 on his way to the Council of Lyons.

Aquinas worked with a strict separation between reason and revelation. What could be known about the world could be found through reason and study. Statements of faith such as the resurrection, purgatory and the immortality of the soul were of the order of revelation. Faith was not unreasonable, however, and a rational defence of belief could be made; Aquinas supported this with his 'proofs' of the existence of God, particularly the cosmological and the teleological arguments. These stated, respectively, that there must be an 'unmoved mover' to begin causation, and that the cosmos is made for a purpose and its design demands the hand of a creator. Aquinas also turned his attention to the eucharist and coined the term 'transubstantiation', meaning that the elements were changed into the body and blood, but only in their underlying, invisible, immeasurable substances and not in their physical accidents, or the things that can be measured.

The doctrine of real presence, the reality of Christ's presence in the consecrated bread and wine of communion, had been affirmed earlier but it was undefined. Aquinas was concerned to defend the real presence, but also to safeguard its spiritual nature when there were debates in the church that understood this in crude terms – for instance, 'did the faithful crunch the body of Christ with their teeth?' His teaching became popular and was adopted as the official Catholic teaching by the Council of Trent after the Reformation.

Aquinas, for all his great learning, had a deep humility. He admitted that the most ignorant peasant woman who knew Christ was more blessed and favoured than the greatest philosopher of old. He also had a mystical experience one day, sensing the glory of God when at prayer in the chapel. After this he said that all he had written was as straw. The truth and mystery of God were greater than the human mind.

Mystics and spiritual movements

Deep and detailed scholarship, debating with ancient philosophers, was one aspect of medieval church life, but mysticism and a more experiential spirituality were also important. In fact, there was a scholarly reaction to the logic of the Schoolmen, which is evident, for example, in the works of the learned Bernard of Clairveaux (1090–1153). He wrote mystical commentaries on Scripture, especially the Song of Songs, about which he wrote eighty-six sermons. There were also monastic and lay movements that encouraged spiritual growth beyond basic religious duties. Texts such as *The Cloud of Unknowing*, an anonymous, fourteenth-century English devotional guide, followed the way of contemplation, as perfected by the monastics with time on their hands dedicated to this goal. They sought to move the soul closer and closer to Jesus by prayer, worship, humility, obedience and inner sanctification.

Richard Rolle (c. 1300–49) of Hampole was another medieval English writer, who experienced a profound conversion and lived as a hermit in the north of England. His works included *The Fire of Love*. He experienced prayer as 'heat, sweetness and song' and he used vivid images for his relationship with the Lord. He describes the sweetness of different types of birdsong and then adds, 'How much more should I sing with great sweetness to Christ my Jesus, that is spouse of my soul.'

A very popular medieval spiritual classic was *The Imitation of Christ* by Thomas à Kempis (1379/80–1471). How much is actually from à Kempis and how much from other brethren of his community is debatable, as their wisdom might have been assembled together. Whatever the case, the text has inspired for many, many years. Thomas lived in an informal lay community, the Congregation of the Common Life, in Holland. This encouraged spiritual renewal and a close walk with Christ. Scriptures were read and meditated upon and Jesus was a living contemporary who spoke in the soul. The way to perfection lay in the road to the cross as a way of giving oneself to God and humbly obeying him by his grace. There is much in that work about the graces of spiritual consolation from the Spirit, through the Word and through the sacraments; thus in chapter one, 'The teaching of Christ excels all the teachings of the Saints; and if a man have His Spirit, he shall find therein a hidden manna. But it so happens that many hear the Gospel frequently and are little affected; because they lack the Spirit of Christ... '[1] We can see how the Scriptures were known and used as rich, devotional material by medievals who had some measure of education.

Wandering preachers

Wandering preachers were another feature of the Middle Ages. They flourished between the twelfth and fourteenth centuries, though they were not always welcomed. One of the most famous, a rich Frenchman called Valdes, gave all his money to the poor in 1175, and lived off donations from those he preached to in the street. He and his followers became popular with the ordinary folk. They did not take monastic vows but simply preached repentance. They became known as Waldesians and were refused permission to preach unless given it by the local clergy, which was never forthcoming. They came to be regarded as heretics in 1179. Their numbers grew and they became more radical, holding to the Bible alone and rejecting many tenets of medieval Catholicism.

Another wandering beggar who gave away his riches was Giovanni Bernardone in 1206. He became known as Francis of Assisi. He was treated with the same suspicion at first, but when he and his followers asked permission from the pope to form an order and to take vows, they were accepted. He worked within the institutional church for renewal and birthed an order of the friars, wandering religious men bound by vows of poverty, obedience and chastity, who were expected to leave the confines of the friary to preach to the poor. They called themselves Friars Minor, suggesting that they saw themselves as the lower levels of society.

A further new order of friars was the Dominicans, founded by Dominic (1170–1221). They were known as Friars Preachers and became involved in countering heresy. Dominic was originally an Augustinian canon in a community at Osma cathedral in Spain. Travelling to Denmark in 1204, he met members of the Albigensians near Toulouse, whose movement was either similar to that of the Cathars or a variant within it. The Cathar heresy was prevalent in parts of Europe at this time; its adherents held to an austere, world-denying lifestyle, and saw the body as inferior to the spirit, rather like the ancient Gnostics. The Albigensians taught dualism and the liberation of the spirit from matter, rather like the ancient Manichees. Dominic felt called to combat heresies such as these by righteous living, prayer and patient teaching and peaceful persuasion. He trained communities of women who lived as austerely as Cathar women, so that they could gain their respect.

When a crusade was declared in 1208 against the Cathars in the South of France Dominic and his followers were not involved in the violence. For the last seven years of his life he established, with the pope's permission, the Dominican order, or the Black Friars; this was a preaching and teaching order, and followed a form of the Augustinian rule. He helped to develop the form of the rosary with its mysteries as it is known today, as an aid to devotion and to assist in teaching the gospel story to the illiterate.

Holy women

Women often played an influential role in medieval church life. As religious figures they had a degree of freedom and could acquire great learning. Mystics and scholars among them made their presence known. For example, Hildegard of Bingen (1098–1179) was abbess firstly at Diessenburg, and later of the Benedictine convent at Rupertsberg, near Bingen in the Rhineland. She wrote her *Scivias* (possibly short for *sciens vias*, 'one who knows ways of expertise or knowledge', thus 'know the way'), which detailed twenty-six visions dealing with morality and enigmatic prophecies. She had a poetic turn of phrase, with a strong sense of the immanence of God. The Holy Spirit was a vital power and an experienced presence in Hildegard's writings, for example in her *De Spiritu Sancto* ('On the Holy Spirit'):

> *Holy Spirit, life that gives life,*
> *moving all things,*
> *rooted in all beings;*
> *you cleanse all things of impurity,*
> *wiping away sins,*
> *and anointing wounds,*
> *this is radiant, laudable life,*
> *awakening and re-awakening*
> *every thing.*

In her *Letter to Abbot Philip*, Hildegard wrote of herself as a tiny feather picked up by the wind and used for God's purposes, showing both a strong humility and a poetic imagination:

A wind blew from a high mountain and, as it passed over ornamented castles and towers, it put into motion a small feather which had no ability of its own to fly but received its movement entirely from the wind. Surely the almighty God arranged this to show what the Divine could achieve through a creature that had no hope of achieving anything by itself.

Her popularity resulted in many stories of miracles and answers to prayer at her tomb, leading to attempts to have her canonized. This was the first time such a lengthy process had been used and it was never completed, leaving her as beatified, the first stage of the process.

Mother Julian of Norwich (c. 1342–1420), one of the first women to leave extant writings in English, was an anchorite at St Julian's Church. An anchorite took a vow to live a solitary monastic life, that of a hermit, but bound to a particular place from whence he or she would never venture. It was a movement in parts of the medieval church, particularly in Norfolk and also in Flanders, which had strong commercial links with that English county. Julian was sought out as a counsellor and intercessor by many. She is known because of her book *The Revelations of Divine Love*. Having fallen into a serious illness, she prayed to receive a revelation of Christ's suffering; she was healed forthwith and then received sixteen 'showings' or visions. These are written down in two versions, a short form and a longer form. The latter was the fruit of years of reflection upon the original. She showed linguistic skill, blending Anglo-Saxon and French idioms with local Norfolk sea imagery – one example is the image of the drops of blood on Christ's head pictured as the scales of a herring.

Hers was a joyful revelation: from the passion and the cross comes redemption and a great love is shown forth for all creation. She saw a tiny hazelnut in the palm of God's hand and realized that this was like the whole of creation to him; we are so infinitesimally small to the transcendent creator, but he loves us profoundly and stooped low to become man. She heard, ' I am the foundation of your praying' and was called to trust in that Love despite all doubts and fears: '... our Lord tenderly teaches us and blessedly calls us, saying in our souls, "Leave me alone, my beloved child, attend to me. I am enough for you, and rejoice in your Saviour and your salvation... " ' Moreover she saw that, in the end, despite sin and judgment, we need not fear for 'All shall be well and all shall be well, and all manner of thing shall be well.'

Julian also spoke of Jesus as a Mother, which sounds at first like modern, feminist theology. This was a tradition among some religious thinkers in the Middle Ages. It used the imagery of Christ as Wisdom, who is personified in the Old Testament as feminine, and also picked up on Jesus' reference to himself as a hen trying to gather his chicks under his wings.

The rise of Islam and the Holy Roman Empire

The rise of Islam took the church, both Western and Eastern, unawares. Muhammad (c. 570–632) had probably intended to take his mission only to the Arabs. By the time of his death and several military campaigns, however, the different Arab tribes were united in the new faith. Muslim expansion probably began by accident as tribes raided the border areas for booty now that they were forbidden from fighting and raiding each other as Muslims. By this time, both the Byzantine and Persian empires were in decline and could not repel the raiders. Opposition crumbled before them and they swept into Palestine, Syria and across North Africa. Islam had to adapt to overseeing an empire, and to teaching and spreading the new faith to new races and peoples. The Qur'an had taught that 'There must be no compulsion in religion' (Sura 2:256) and special protection and tolerance was allowed for the 'People of the Book', Jews and Christians. They had to pay a tax, the *jizya*, as compensation for not serving in the army. Life under Muslim control could be preferable to Byzantine rule for some, as the monophysites or Nestorians and other, more heterodox groups were tolerated equally as Christians rather than being treated as heretics. Generally speaking, though Christian proselytizing was forbidden, their holy places and churches were protected. (When Jerusalem fell to the Muslims the patriarch welcomed them to the Church of the Holy Sepulchre. Their leader refused to unroll his mat and offer prayers there in case his followers thought he had claimed it for Islam.)

Muslim scholars rediscovered the Greek philosophers and passed on many lost texts to the West, and their cities could be centres of civilization – for example Granada or Cordoba in Spain.

Relationships between Christians and Muslims varied from place to place in the medieval period, ranging from great toleration and prosperity to control and limitation. Outright persecution was rare as this was forbidden by the Qur'an – fighting against the People of the Book was permitted only in self-defence. Inevitably, given human nature, it did sometimes happen, and even in peaceful situations some felt that they were now a minority in an alien culture. Their numbers shrank, and the church of North Africa, for example, once a centre of Christian civilization and learning, was swept aside by Muslim culture. Churches gradually closed or fell into disuse and second- and third-generation Christians converted to enjoy the opportunities of the new culture fully. The largest Christian community remained in Egypt, the Coptic Church.

A weakened Byzantine empire and the rising power of Islam acted as a spur to bring more cohesion and unity to the emerging, rival nation states of Europe. Muslim advance beyond Spain had been stopped by Charles Martel at Tours in 732, but concern for abiding security remained. The rising star was Charlemagne (c. 742–814) of the Franks who fought campaign after campaign, subjecting parts of Europe from Lombard and Bavaria to part of Spain, including Barcelona. He introduced a strong, centralized form of government with itinerant royal legates. He also encouraged ecclesiastical reform and gave his protection and patronage to the church. On Christmas Day in the year 800, Pope Leo III crowned him as the first 'Holy Roman Emperor', in an act which showed that the papacy in the West was a powerbroker and a kingmaker. The restoration of the emperor of the West was an attempt to unify the nations and create a strong, centralized defence against Muslim expansion. This new emperor was something of a rival to the Byzantine emperor, and this caused more strain between East and West.

Crusades

The Holy Land was a political tinderbox then, as now, and the crusades began to liberate the Christian holy places from Muslim control. The first crusade was preached by Pope Urban II in 1095 after petitions from the Byzantine emperor for help and protection against Muslim expansion. It resulted in the reconquest of Jerusalem in 1099. Urban had condemned any selfish motive in going on crusade; it was for love of God and for the liberation of the Holy Land alone. However, in some cases the victorious crusaders sought power and land and eastern kingdoms were set up in what became known as 'Outremer', the area 'across the sea'. When Jerusalem was taken, the crusaders massacred Muslims, Jews and Orthodox Christians in the holy city, so that blood flowed in the streets. This sacrilege has worsened relations with Muslims to this day. Tensions mounted with the Orthodox, too, following the crusaders' expulsion of the patriarch from Antioch.

The second crusade in 1146, encouraged by Bernard of Clairveaux, was a military failure. The third crusade in 1189 involved the colourful historical characters Richard the Lionheart and Saladin, and resulted in a stalemate and truce, ensuring the rights of Christian pilgrims. A fourth crusade in 1204 got no further than Constantinople when the crusaders sacked the city and killed many. This caused more bitterness and separation between Rome and the Orthodox than the Great Schism of 1054. Various smaller crusades carried on in both the East and the West, but the emphasis turned towards combating heresy nearer home, for example in the campaign against the Cathars in the South of France.

Wyclif and the Lollards

England also had wandering preachers, called the Lollards. They followed the lead of the priest John Wyclif, an Oxford don of the fourteenth century who attacked the corruption of the papacy of the time. There had been rival popes for years amidst power struggles between the papal claimants at Avignon and Rome. Wyclif rejected the authority of an immoral pope and gradually turned to the Bible as the real source of authority. Other traditions of the church were to be valued only if they were consonant with Scripture. To mix human traditions on a par with the Word was to ruin and weaken the church. He spoke of the doctrine of 'dominion', whereby all authority is from God and those who wield it must act responsibly and morally. He translated the Bible into English and his lay preachers (nicknamed Lollards, meaning 'babblers') spread his ideas and taught the Scriptures.

The church hierarchy was enraged – they feared that an unauthorized translation of the Bible was dangerous and could contain many errors and heresy. The English nobility, however, were discontented with the power of the church and they were prepared to protect Wyclif for a time. Then, more radically, Wyclif attacked the idea that the eucharist was changed into the body and blood of Christ. By the fourteenth century, the way that this was commonly understood was transubstantiation, a doctrine derived from the writings of Thomas Aquinas. By attacking this concept Wyclif felt that he was attacking the power of the priests who were set apart as possessing the power to make the change in the elements of bread and wine. This, however, was too much for the establishment and he lost much support. He had to leave Oxford but he continued to live and teach quietly at Lutterworth, where he died in 1384.

Wyclif was condemned as a heretic after his death; his body was exhumed, and his remains were burnt at the stake. The Lollard movement forced the hand of the authorities to introduce severe penalties for heresy akin to those on the continent – death by hanging or burning. After Wyclif's death, a law was passed stating that whoever read the Scriptures in English should forfeit land, chattels, goods and life. Despite these penalties, Lollard congregations continued for many years after Wyclif's death, particularly in East Anglia, London, Buckinghamshire, Norfolk and Suffolk.

Jan Hus

Wyclif also influenced a reform movement in Prague. Bohemian students came to Oxford to study when King Richard II married Princess Anne of Bohemia in 1382. They took his ideas back home and Jan Hus (c. 1372–1415), the rector of Prague University, championed the cause of reform until he himself was condemned. Hus had been a preacher in Czech at the Bethlehem Chapel in Prague when Wyclif's writings were first coming into the country. Hus was impressed by the way these works both attacked the morals of the clergy and questioned the power of earthly hierarchies. At first the archbishop of Prague supported him, but his position became increasingly untenable after the university condemned many of Wyclif's ideas in 1403.

Hus's sermons provoked hostility and were denounced at Rome in 1407. He was protected by Czech nobility and remained secure for a time when the Czechs took control of the university. He then wrote his magnum opus, *De Ecclesia*, in 1413, showing a great dependence upon Wyclif. He appealed against his excommunication to a forthcoming general council of the church at Constance. Promised safe conduct, once the trial had begun he was imprisoned by first the Dominicans, then the Franciscans and the secular authorities. He died at the stake in 1415.

Hus's story highlights the intellectual and religious ferment towards the close of the medieval period and the desire to question traditions and authority in the light of Scripture.

Attempts at reunion with the Orthodox

An attempt to heal the breach between the Eastern and Western churches almost worked in 1438–49 at the Council of Florence. There had been several efforts by the Byzantine emperors to renew contacts with the papacy, especially with the threat of Islam at their doorstep. Rome had suffered its own schism with rival popes and when this was finally settled with the election of Martin V in 1417, the issue of reunion with the East was also raised. With the pressure of the Ottoman Turks on the Byzantines, the Byzantine emperor was more than ready to listen. The emperor and the patriarch attended the council with various bishops and scholars, including representatives of the other patriarchs.

The four issues of purgatory, the *filioque* clause, papal supremacy and the use of unleavened bread were on the agenda. Some clarifications resulted, and the language used to express the four concepts was careful, with perhaps deliberate ambiguities. For example, the council agreed firstly that Christians should understand that papal supremacy was in the ancient canons of the church that everybody followed. Secondly, purgatory was to be taught unequivocally – it was a development of doctrine and devotional practice that had grown in the West following the schism. In the third place, priests would be free to use leavened or unleavened bread. Finally, the procession of the Holy Spirit was couched in terms that made it more acceptable to the Byzantines.

The emperor held to the union as did most of the delegates with him. Those left behind in Constantinople rejected it, whether dignitaries, clergy or laity. The Russian church followed suit. Delegates fled for their lives or repented and retired to a monastery. They feared harassment and violence should they return home without due care. The emperor could not enforce the union without causing great persecution. His will was not in line with that of most of his people. Eventually, with the fall of Constantinople in 1453, the Ottomans upheld the rejection of the union – it was politically expedient.

Inquisition

An inquisition procedure was established in 1231, under the direction of Rome, principally to deal with the problem of the Cathars. The Cathars rejected the body as inferior to the spirit and demanded celibacy of every full member ('the parfait' or 'perfect'). A series of wars tried to eradicate the heresy when in the thirteenth century Pope Innocent ordered a crusade, not against the Muslims but to the south of France where most Cathars dwelt. The accused were offered a chance to repent, and, for those who did, a penance such as fasting or pilgrimage was imposed. Torture was condoned in 1252, as this was a standard means of exacting 'truth' in medieval law. Death penalties were rarer than has been imagined, though fines, imprisonment and confiscation of property were more common. The church could not sentence to death but it could hand over a person to the power of the state, who would execute.

Though the eradication of the Cathar heresy was the main aim of the Roman Inquisition, after its decline the system continued to deal with various charges of heresy. The activity of this arm of the church waxed and waned over the next few centuries. It was occasionally encouraged and had activities restored by various popes and prelates. The original motive might have been to protect souls from error that would lead them from saving truth but this became entangled with power.

After stemming the heresy of the Cathars, the Inquisition turned, in the fourteenth century, to examining the religious orders. The religious communities were independent of the local bishop and if they were corrupted, they could do great evil in the sight of the establishment. The principal orders who were attacked were the Templars and the spiritual Franciscans, the *fraticelli*, who were seen as extreme in that they rejected ownership of all property. The Templars were accused of worshipping an idol, Baphomet, but in practice they were probably feared for their wealth and influence as the bankers of Europe. Many would have benefited from their removal from the scene. Speculation abounds about the real reasons that they were condemned; the Inquisition only started the trials and then handed them over to the secular authorities. One of the chief inquisitors of the time, Bernard Gui, was baffled by the contrary evidence. It was a complicated case that some thought was contrived because of the wealth and influence the Templars held at this time.

The celebrity case of the fifteenth century was Jeanne d'Arc, the Maid of Orleans, and this was a trial full of political manoeuvring. It is worth noting that just over a century separated the celebrity cases of the Templars (1307–14) and the Maid of Orleans (1430). Such affairs were not everyday events.

The Inquisition led by Rome faded in importance after the fifteenth century, though it was periodically revived by later popes. Spain, however, relaunched the Inquisition in its domain towards the end of the fifteenth century for fear of the Moors and the Jews. Many *converso*s (people of other faiths who had converted to Christianity) from both camps came under suspicion. The Spanish Inquisition was more in the hands of the state. Here there were more cases of torture and brutality, as well as discrimination – the Jews were forced to wear a yellow star. Still, lists of punishments show that actual executions were few – fifteen from 1575 to 1610 and eight from 1648 to 1794. The most common report was of the imposition of a penance followed by imprisonment or confiscation of goods.

The power of the Inquisition, whether under Rome or Spain, declined in the Age of Enlightenment, which started in the late seventeenth century, and with the rise of more independent, nation states.

In conclusion

This ramble through the countryside of the medieval church has seen many movements, individuals, rituals and power struggles. No doubt there was a great deal of nominalism and superstition when a society forced people to believe and allowed little debate. We also hear of life-changing encounters and conversions such as the visions of Hildegard or Julian, and the songs of Rolle. Some sought to renew the church from within the established institution; others felt forced out of it and challenged many aspects of its structure and teaching in the name of the gospel. This ferment of renewal and a desire for some degree of reform was to bubble up in the sixteenth century in the Reformation. At this time, issues such as the primacy of the Bible, the role of grace and the place of faith and works in justification were to come to the fore. They were not sudden events for there had been a debate taking place for many years. The medieval church had strict controls, but there were rival schools of thought on many issues. When certain doctrines were undefined, many opinions were tolerated and could flourish. The existence of the different religious orders gave a variety of styles of worship and teaching. The rise of literacy and a merchant class brought new challenges and insights to medieval society. The sixteenth century was to be a time of immense upheaval.

Timeline

632	Death of Muhammad
731	Bede completed *A History of the English Church and People*
732	Charles Martel stopped the Muslim advance at Tours
800	Charlemagne crowned Holy Roman Emperor by the pope
11th–13th centuries	The four main crusades. The fourth ended at Constantinople in 1204 when the city was sacked
1054	Great Schism between East and West
1061	Lady Richeldis of Walsingham had her vision
1095	First crusade
1146	Second crusade
1189	Third crusade
1204	Fourth crusade
1274	Death of Thomas Aquinas
1305–76	Pope in exile at Avignon

1378–1417	The 'Great Schism' when there were rival popes
1384	Death of John Wyclif
1420	Death of Julian of Norwich
1471	Death of Thomas à Kempis

At a glance

- Medieval Europe had a set of rhythms and festivities that supplied the spiritual needs of most people. It was a vast, established, interconnected society; people were baptized into it and they left it through Christian funeral rites. Holy days abounded and the monasteries dispensed education, health care and charity. Tensions were evident in the use of Latin as literacy increased, and in the corruption in parts of the church.

- Popular devotions such as the rosary and pilgrimages, with impressively decorated churches, helped laity who knew no Latin.

- The rebirth of learning in the renaissance, and the rediscovery of classical texts via Muslim scholars, led to the rise of the universities. The scholar clerics were known as Scholastics or Schoolmen; of these the greatest abiding influence was Thomas Aquinas.

- Experiential spirituality was also pursued through mystics and visionaries such as Hildegard, Julian of Norwich and Richard Rolle and through the devotions of lay communities, as found in *The Imitation of Christ*.

- Wandering preachers sought to radicalize the church and to call it to renewal. Some, like Valdes, rejected the hierarchy; others worked within it, such as Francis and Dominic who formed the Friars Minor and the Blackfriars respectively.

- The rise of Islam in the East shook the Christian world. Charlemagne was crowned Holy Roman Emperor in 800 by Pope Leo III, in an attempt to reform the Western Roman empire by giving it a secular figurehead as well as a spiritual one.
- The crusades ran from the eleventh to the thirteenth century, though other campaigns dragged on across Europe against Muslims and heretical groups such as the Cathars.
- The Roman Inquisition was formed in the thirteenth century to settle the menace of the Cathars, but it worked sporadically to counter heresy in religious communities and individuals. The Spanish Inquisition was created later to deal with Moors and Jews, even those who had converted and were nevertheless seen as a threat.

Endnotes

1. Thomas à Kempis, *The Imitation of Christ*, trans. Leo Sherley-Price, *The Imitation of Christ*, London: Penguin Classics, 1952, p. 27.

7. The Reformation

In the sixteenth century the Western church split apart. The desire for reform was increasing and broke out spontaneously across Europe in the hands of different teachers. There was corruption in the church as people had known for some time; the scandal of having rival popes for a time was a cause of concern as was the immoral lifestyle of some prelates. It was said of Pope Innocent VIII (1432–92), 'Look at all his children. Well may Rome call him "Father"!' Until this time most people were happy with the worship and sacraments of the church and only isolated individuals had risen up to challenge the status quo. A number of factors conspired to take matters much further in the sixteenth century with more independent nation states, wider education and the printing press. Nevertheless, no one expected to see the church break up. There was a desire to return to the sources – the Scriptures newly read in Greek and the early fathers – and simply to renew. Long-standing discussions and debates came to the fore and, in a new socio-economic context, dissention spread and had unforeseen effects. The rise of the major Western denominations, such as the Anglicans, Lutherans and Presbyterians, can be traced to this time of upheaval and division.

The rebirth of learning

A couple of centuries of trade with the East, crusades and newly discovered manuscripts had opened up the West to a rebirth of learning, the renaissance. This affected architecture, politics, art and philosophy. The ancient wisdom of the Greeks, Aristotle especially, had been recovered. It was a creative world of concepts and new ideas with a rising merchant class that was bringing education and literacy out of the upper classes and the cloisters. The study of Greek, a direct result of the renaissance and the rediscovery of the classical world, enabled more people to read the New Testament in the original, rather than Jerome's Latin Vulgate translation. Soon afterwards came the Council of Florence in 1439 when an attempt was made to reunite with the Eastern church. This failed, and Constantinople fell in 1453. A number of Greek-speaking clergy and monks had travelled west and were given the patronage of the new middle classes to tutor them in Greek so that they could read the classics and the New Testament.

A final fruit of this rebirth of learning was the invention of the printing press by William Caxton in 1474, which revolutionized communication. Pamphlets and posters could travel quickly and relatively inexpensively compared to the days of paying a cleric to write out a manuscript by hand.

Freedom of thought?

The rising middle classes and the new education caused a desire for freedom of thought and opinion, and a corresponding desire in politics. This was a time of shift, of the continuing rise of nation states, when the power of the pope could be challenged. The church and the state were still intertwined in Europe and dissent could be charged with heresy, which was punishable in various ways. The Inquisition was still in force, though more so in certain areas than others. The old order was creaking, but there was no great or general desire to throw off the church, merely to reform it to some extent, to rid it of hypocrisy.

The Bible and buildings

Erasmus (c. 1469–1536), the Dutch scholar from Rotterdam and a good friend of Thomas More (1478–1535), published a Greek translation of the New Testament and began to criticize certain inaccuracies of the Vulgate. He pointed out that when Jesus preached repentance, this was a change of heart and not a list of prayers and minor punishments to be prescribed to the sinner – the Vulgate's 'to do penance' had come to mean the latter in the medieval church. Marriage in Ephesians 5:32 is a 'mystery' in the Greek rather than a *sacramentum* as in the Latin. These sorts of differences might seem small – much in the Vulgate stood the test of time and it was a scholarly, valiant effort to put the Scriptures into Latin. However, it raised doubts in the late medieval mind, for people had assumed that the whole panoply of medieval church doctrine was right there in the New Testament. Some of it was not as clearly present as they had assumed.

Erasmus and others in the renaissance humanist movement wanted a peaceful reform. ('Humanist' here refers to those who wanted to advance the new learning and the arts; they were not unbelievers.) He satirized the behaviour of clergy as Chaucer had done years before and longed for reliable, sanctioned translations of the Scriptures in the vernacular: 'Do you think the Scriptures are only fit for the perfumed?' he asked.

The patronage of the arts was costly for Rome. Pope Nicholas V had made the holy city the patron of the arts, collecting paintings and manuscripts. In 1506, Julian II laid the foundation of St Peter's basilica. This was going to be expensive and the

Reformation proper began when Pope Leo X sought to raise taxes for the costly building programme. He had a novel idea, which would prove to cost more than the revenue it brought in. Indulgencies were, and still are, a remittance of the temporal effects of sin. By partaking in some prescribed devotional act – the rosary, masses, pilgrimages, for example – a sinner received an indulgence that was either partial or total and reduced any penances that needed to be undertaken. This was seen as in the gift of the church from the rich treasury of mercies from Christ and the merits of the saints that had accrued. It was indulgent – a free act of grace and mercy. This concept was generally accepted at first; however objections were raised when the pope started to *sell* indulgencies. A gift of money for St Peter's was as good as doing something devotional, for oneself or the deceased. This traffic was more pronounced in northern Europe, it seems, and one seller, Tetzel, was particularly crass. He sang, 'When a coin in the coffer rings, a soul from purgatory springs.' This was to be the tinderbox that started the European Reformation.

Luther's protest

Behaviour such as Tetzel's caused Martin Luther (1483–1546), an Augustinian monk and lecturer in theology, to nail 95 Theses – points of protest and debate – to the cathedral door in Wittenberg in 1517. This was a normal staging post and notice board for announcements and discussions, and Luther meant it as nothing more than a local, academic discussion. However, his action lit the fuse that set off the Reformation. The Theses themselves contain little apart from criticizing the sale of indulgencies and the improper use of power by the pope. There is no radical Reformation statement about Mary, the saints, the mass or purgatory, for example. However, there are seeds here that germinated later. Luther attacked the sale of indulgencies and also the poverty of knowledge about the treasury of the church among common people. He also, significantly, reminded his readers that the true treasures are the gospel and lamented that more time was spent preaching about an indulgence than about the Word itself: 'They are enemies of Christ and the pope who forbid altogether the preaching of the Word of God in some churches in order that indulgencies might be preached in others' (Thesis 53). He also criticized the pope for building St Peter's with the money of the poor rather than with his own.

The storm had broken so much that by 1520 Luther had been excommunicated and in 1521 he was called to give an account of himself to the Diet of Worms where he famously declared, after his defence, 'Here I stand; I can do no other.' The Elector of Saxony, a supporter of Luther's, gave him protection or his life might have been shortened. He was hidden in Wartburg castle for a year and given a false identity of Junker George. People assumed he must be dead. During this time he worked on his translation of the Bible into German, an outstanding literary achievement after the poorer and incomplete versions which had been in circulation. As his followers grew stronger in Wittenberg, he returned to take control.

Luther's revolt against ecclesiastical authority was to have a side effect. Other issues came into the open from the disaffected populace and a peasants' revolt spread from 1524–25. At first Luther sympathized but as the perpetrators' violence increased he wrote a pamphlet against them stating that it was the state's duty to stop them and to think nothing ill of killing them, for 'nothing can be more devilish than a rebel... ' The Catholic hierarchy would have smiled at the irony of the situation, for they were saying the same about Luther.

The revolt was over by the time his pamphlet appeared and the rulers exacted a terrible revenge, massacring thousands of peasants. He deeply regretted what he had written in haste, and side-stepped politics from then on, creating a neutrality that affected Lutheranism for centuries to come.

Luther gradually developed more Reformed ideas, abandoning belief in purgatory and seeing the preaching of the Word as the primary element in ministry, rather than the sacraments. However, Luther was always the most Catholic minded of the Reformers. He still held to the perpetual virginity of the Virgin Mary, for example, and maintained a belief in the real presence in the eucharist that was not so far from that of Rome – namely consubstantiation, whereby the substance of the body and blood co-exist with those of bread and wine. He also sanctioned the use of church decoration and vestments.

He went on to write three major texts, *The Babylonian Captivity of the Church*, *The Freedom of a Christian Man*, and *To the Christian Nobility of the German Nation*. This last work urged princes and nations to seize control of the church and reform it themselves. Here we see the continuing rising power and influence of the nation state. Interestingly, there seems to have been a following for Luther's works, printed under anonymous authorship, in parts of southern Europe. Many were asking the kind of questions Luther raised.

Luther faced the question of religious vows and celibacy personally when twelve nuns arrived in Wittenberg seeking sanctuary and allegiance to Luther. Three returned to their homes, and Luther sought husbands for the other nine. There was one he could not house, Catherine, and so he took her into his home as his wife. There are touching references in his letters, describing how he experienced married life, adjusting to 'wak[ing] up in the morning and find[ing] a pair of pigtails on the pillow which were not there before.'[1] In his later work, *Concerning Married Life*, he writes of the lowly task of washing nappies and caring for infants: 'the father open his eyes, looks at these lowly, distasteful and despised things and knows that they are adorned with divine approval as with the most precious gold and silver...'[2]

Zurich, Geneva and Canterbury

Ulrich Zwingli (1484–1531) won a debate about religion at Zurich in 1522 when he was called upon in the defence of a printer who had eaten a sausage during Lent. The bishop's deputy stood head to head with this reforming priest, who had watched the man eat the meat. Zwingli won the debate. It was a silly flash point, but one that opened the doors to reform. Zwingli appealed to the Scriptures alone and saw no mention of Lent or forbidden foods therein. He was invited to lead the reform of the church in Switzerland and he was far more radical than Luther, removing all ornamentation and even the minster organ. Communion now took place around a plain table with a minister in plain clothes distributing the sacrament. The monasteries were dissolved and their wealth was used for the poor.

John Calvin (1509–64) was brought up in Picardy and intended upon an ecclesiastical career. He received the tonsure aged twelve and went to study in Paris, but developed doubts about his vocation as a priest in 1527. He then studied law at Orleans and Bourges where he came under the influence of a circle of Protestants. In 1533 he had a religious experience which convinced him of a call to restore the church to its original purity. He fled persecution in Paris in 1535 to Basle, where he wrote his *Institutes of the Christian Religion*, the first edition appearing in Latin in 1536, though throughtout his life, subsequent editions saw continuous improvement and reworking. These gave a thorough analysis of the Reformed views and his developing middle way between figures such as Zwingli and Luther on certain points of doctrine, as well as his distinctive teaching about predestination. He was invited to teach at Geneva but was expelled over his severe rules for receiving communion. He lectured at Strasburg and ministered to the French congregation, where he met Martin Bucer (1491–1551) who influenced new editions of the *Institutes*. He was invited back to Geneva in 1541 and ran a form of theocracy for the next fourteen years through a series of ordinances governed by the four classes of pastors, doctors, elders and deacons. There was a consistory of ministers and laypeople which acted as a moral tribunal and people were punished for unbelief or heresy. Entertainments such as dancing and gaming were prohibited and Calvin's opponents were arrested, tortured and executed.

By 1555 opposition had died out, and Calvin continued unchallenged until his death. He wrote to Protector Somerset in England in 1548 advising on the changes necessary to the church in England, as well as welcoming English refugees from Mary Tudor's reign in 1555. In fact, of all the Reformation movements, Calvinism was the most international, with its émigrés and visitors seeking instruction and inspiration. One of these was John Knox (c. 1513–72), the Scottish Reformer. He preached in Edward VI's England, being the king's chaplain, but fled to the continent upon the accession of Mary Tudor. He met Calvin at Geneva and declared the place to be 'the most perfect school of Christ that ever was in the earth since the days of the Apostles.' By the close of the sixteenth century, there were Calvinist congregations in the Netherlands, Scotland and in France with the powerful French Protestant, or Huguenot, community. It even seemed possible, for a time, that France might be won for Protestantism as the Huguenots, though a substantial minority, were largely made up of the nobility and the educated classes.

The Netherlands became a place of toleration as Calvinist leaders and princes campaigned for freedom of religious expression in the face of opposition from their Spanish overlords. In Scotland, Knox led the people into a Calvinist system of worship when the Scottish parliament rejected papal authority in 1560. He preached the moral duty of Christians to refuse state authority when it was unrighteous and advocated self-defence when persecuted. In this he disagreed with Calvin.

Meanwhile, Henry VIII was declared head of the church in England in 1534 over issues of inheritance and his desire to take a new wife. The bishops had only agreed to this on condition that a clause was added to his Act of Supremacy that stated, 'as far as the law of Christ allows'. Henry also saw the opportunity to seize more power and wealth for himself from monasteries and church lands. This was a partial Reformation for, except for removing the pope's authority, in many matters of faith and practice he retained the church as it had been, passing the Act of Six Articles to this effect in 1539, although near the end of his reign he allowed some parts of the liturgy in the vernacular such as the Lord's Prayer. Thomas Cranmer, the archbishop of Canterbury (1489–1556), gradually absorbed continental Reformed views and was in contact with various clerics. He produced the *Book of Common Prayer* during the reign of Edward VI, the 1549 edition being more Catholic in content, and the 1552 book more Protestant.

'Protestant'?

The term 'Protestant' came into use in 1529 when a diet ordered the six German Reformed princes and the fourteen cities under Reformed influence to revert to the Catholic faith. They joined forces and wrote a 'Protestation'. Philip of Hesse led them in a military alliance and toleration was achieved only by the Peace of Augsburg in 1555. Such an uprising and national level of resistance would have been unthinkable some years earlier. The Reformation took shape partly as a political movement as well as a theological one.

Counter Reformation

A number of Catholic clergy and laity saw the need for reform but in much gentler terms that the Protestants. The Catholic Church needed to tighten discipline and morals in certain areas. Ignatius Loyola (c. 1491–1556) formed the Society of Jesus, the Jesuits, in 1539. Loyola had been converted in heart when reading the Gospels and lives of the saints as he lay recovering from a wound after a battle. Before this he had sought a military career. He spent a year in retreat, doing penance, reading and experiencing visions before going to Jerusalem on mission. Rejected by the Franciscans, he spent twelve years teaching in universities and gathering a circle of close followers. During this time he wrote his *Spiritual Exercises*, a programme for a retreat that examines the soul and speaks of heaven, hell and the need for obedience to the church. The friends resolved to go back to Jerusalem, but failed to organize this. They turned instead to the pope and offered themselves in his service. Paul III gave them permission to form an order and they were known as the Society of Jesus or the Jesuits.

The Jesuits were seen as a group of spiritual soldiers, a task force to counter the Reformation with their orthodox teaching and exemplary holiness. Members of the order became dedicated missionaries, travelling to the Far East, to China, Japan and India. The most famous of these men was Francis Xavier (1506–52), one of the original Jesuits and close friends of Loyola. He travelled to the East Indies, and then to Goa in India, making this his headquarters. He landed in Japan in 1549 and mastered the language, founding a church there. In 1552, having returned to Goa, he set out for China but fell ill on an island before entering the country.

The Jesuits had begun the Counter Reformation, a vigorous attempt to win back hearts to the Catholic Church and to clean up their own act. Many outstanding clergy and religious people were at work in this period, such as Francis de Sales (1567–1622), Bishop of Geneva, who wrote on the love of God, producing the spiritual classics *Introduction to the Devout Life* and *Treatise on the Love of God*.

Philip Neri (1515–95) was known as 'the Apostle of Rome'. In 1544, after a period of intense prayer in the catacomb of St Sebastiano, he experienced an ecstasy in which he believed his heart had been miraculously enlarged as he felt a holy fire of love, of the Holy Spirit, enter him. He ran the Confraternity of the Holy Trinity for many years tending to pilgrims and convalescents, and then began conferences for clergy and boys, who studied Scripture and prayed together. The Oratory movement came from these and was formally recognized by Gregory XIII in 1575. These were renewal meetings, and he was known for his gentleness and his joy.

Theresa of Avila (1515–82) sought to restore the primitive and stricter Rule of Life for her Carmelite sisters. This was the Discalced order, meaning 'without shoes' (i.e. wearing sandals) and their way was more rigorous than that of others in many ways. Her counsellor and friend was John of the Cross (1542–91). His poetic imagination produced spiritual classics such as *The Dark Night of the Soul* and *The Ascent of Mount Carmel*. Fascinated by the Song of Songs and the search for the Beloved, he sought God through love when all other senses and understandings failed.

Regensburg and Trent

Pope Paul III saw the need for a measure of change when he came to power in 1539 and he appointed reforming cardinals such as Gasparo Contarini (1483–1542), who was dispatched to meet with representatives of the Reformers at the Colloquy of Regensburg.

The leading Reformer there was Philip Melanchthon (1497–1560), who took over Luther's movement upon his death. Both men were concerned for peace and desired reunion. Contarini had remarked to Melanchthon, 'How great will be the fruit of unity, and how profound the gratitude of all mankind.'

The two men made much headway on the issue of justification by faith but could not agree on papal authority and transubstantiation. Both were criticized upon their return; the Lutherans rejected the compromises about justification and Contarini was suspected of heresy by his rival Cardinal Carafa.

Contarini had had a personal conversion akin to Luther and was thus sympathetic to much that the Augustinian had sought to achieve. A number of churchmen were in this position but sought to stay within the church and reform it from within. Another such cardinal was Reginald Pole, who wrote on justification and sought to balance the views of both sides, allowing grace to work through the Scriptures as well as the church and the sacraments. Pole was nearly elected pope during this period, but missed the mark by one vote.

Pope Paul III called the Council of Trent to address the question of reform and schism. This started to convene in 1545 and met periodically until 1558, when it was halted under the new pope, Paul IV, formerly the reactionary Cardinal Carafa. He abandoned the council and tried to take matters into his own hands until his death in 1559. The Council of Trent met again to complete its work in 1562–63. It addressed the issue of priestly training, establishing the seminary system, and affirmed Catholic doctrine with regard to the seven sacraments and purgatory. Transubstantiation was now confirmed as official Catholic teaching about the eucharist.

There was a recognition that the Scriptures needed to be available in the vernacular but with translations that carefully avoided what were seen as Reformed errors. Any authorized translations were based upon the Vulgate, which remained the standard text. In 1582 an English translation of the New Testament was published at the college at Douai; the Old Testament followed in 1609, by which time the college had moved to Rheims.

Justification by faith

This was, perhaps, the central issue of the Reformation. Luther had struggled with the system of penances and devotions and could find no inner peace. His conscience constantly troubled him. When he read the New Testament in Greek he saw ideas with fresh eyes. He understood Paul as saying that the righteousness of God is ours in Christ as a gift, a 'sweet exchange' as a bride takes on the wealth and title of her husband at her marriage, whatever her previous state of poverty. It could not be earned by works. He felt loved and accepted and declared, 'I felt myself reborn. I had looked through the gates of Paradise.'

Key to his exposition was that each of us is *simul justus et peccator* (justified and sinner at the same time). By this he meant that Christ's righteousness is imputed to believers as by a legal fiction; it is not their own righteousness. There was, of course, regeneration and sanctification – the work of the Holy Spirit within the soul. This was the impartation of grace for the Reformers, the inward transformation and work within the soul once Christ's external act of justification had been accepted. Calvin, Zwingli and others followed Luther's theology here. The problem was that medieval theology had used one term – *justificatio* – for all three (justification, regeneration and sanctification). Catholic teaching said that by grace we are saved, but that this is imparted (not just imputed) to the believer at baptism and grows as they obey and receive the sacraments. Grace becomes habitual, a part of our lives.

The Schoolmen debated this. Which came first, the *acceptatio* or the *infusio*? The *acceptatio* was our acceptance by God through the righteousness of Christ; the *infusio* was the infusion of grace into the regenerate soul, sanctifying the believer in an initial act and also in an ongoing process. Sanctification was of a piece with justification in the Catholic mind as an ongoing affair. Aquinas argued that the *infusio* came first, after which we were accepted; John Duns Scotus (c. 1266–1308) had claimed that it was the *acceptatio*, basing this on covenant theology. On the basis of God's promise in Christ, and what Christ has done, we are accepted and the work of infusion is simultaneous.

Really this was splitting hairs, and no one had ever sought to separate these concepts before. The problem was that the Reformers did divide the two, and spoke of justification *sola fides*, by 'faith alone'. Rome would not agree to this for justification could not be so apart from the evidence of good works and habitual (i.e. infused) grace. The Coucil of Trent rejected *sola fides*, arguing that by grace we are saved; salvation cannot be earned but by grace we persevere and grow habitually in holiness. Claiming to be saved finally and fully in this life is a nonsense as a process of sanctification is at work. Neither should anyone presume that they will finish the race; they could lapse and apostasize. Thus Catholics speak of the grace of final perseverance.

Some of this dispute rested upon misunderstandings and different terminology. The Protestant distinction between *iustificatio* and *regeneratio*, justification and regeneration, introduced a fundamental discontinuity into the Western theological tradition where none had existed before.

Sola Scriptura

The concept of the *sola scriptura*, or 'the Scriptures alone', was the other touchstone of the Reformation. Humanists such as Erasmus had desired to return to the sources, and reading the Greek New

Testament had opened up many issues anew. They had not intended to go so far as accepting Scripture alone, however, and this became a uniquely Reformed position. If something was not in the Bible it was questionable or to be rejected. When some church leaders were seen as compromised, it is understandable how Scripture could seem to be a reliable guide and authority. Nevertheless, the *sola scriptura* principle could not settle all disputes as the Reformers soon saw. Luther argued that anything forbidden by Scripture should be rejected, but that anything else was permissible if it was not explicitly prohibited. Hence he encouraged ornamentation in church and the singing of hymns. The other Reformers removed all decoration and only said or chanted psalms at first.

The Catholic position, confirmed by the Council of Trent, is that the New Testament might contain the seeds of ideas which germinated later with developing insight and tradition, under the guidance of the Holy Spirit. Tradition is seen as a living stream that includes the Scriptures and various traditions of the apostles and the early church. Revelation is to be found in both; the Word of God comes through both.

Sola scriptura could not satisfy the issue of how the sacrament of the eucharist worked. Was it a symbolic memorial or a real presence? Luther argued for consubstantiation where the substance of the body and blood existed alongside that of bread and wine; Zwingli rejected this, arguing that the body of Christ was ascended and in heaven. The eucharist was thus a symbolic meal, pointing to something greater. The two met at Marburg in 1529 to try to settle the matter. Luther simply repeated the dominical (i.e. those of the Lord) words from the Gospels. What Jesus said was the truth. 'This is my body... this is my blood.' Zwingli could not agree, seeing these words as symbolic. No agreement was reached. Calvin tried to tread a middle path between the two. He saw eucharistic presence as dynamic. The presence of Christ was alongside the bread and wine when given to the faithful communicant; there was no sense of it being 'in' the elements or of their undergoing any substantial change.

Baptism is another case in point. Most of the Reformers followed the line that infants of Christian parents should be baptized. They were still living in a Christian society where that was the expected norm. The New Testament does not explicitly teach this, and some began to question it. Some more radical followers of Zwingli led by Conrad Grebel argued for believers' baptism and rebaptized their members in the river. They became known as 'Anabaptists', 'rebaptizers' and were regarded as serious heretics. Zwingli had some of them drowned as punishment to fit the crime. The case for believers' baptism was seen as a radical stance that threatened to undermine much of the social order. It was not helped by the fact that it was practised by the followers of the radical Reformer Thomas Münzer (c. 1490–1525), who preached social change and the overthrow of government and sought to reintroduce a pure style of Christianity. Münzer was arrested and executed after he allied himself with a peasants' revolt in Germany.

More moderate people were hounded for their Anabaptist beliefs and there are moving accounts of their trials and martyrdoms, collected in the seventeenth-century *Martyr's Mirror*. By 1526, groups of them had settled in Mikulov in Czechoslovakia under the protection of the radical Lutheran Leonhard von Lichtenstein. Here they found stability, tolerance and prosperity for a time. The community split into two over the issues of pacifism and also communitarian sharing. The more radical leaders were executed; one was whipped, had brandy poured into his wounds and was then set alight. The pacifist Thomas Menno became a minister in 1536 and the name 'Mennonite' stuck to many Anabaptist groups. Some found their way to the New World which was opening up in the seventeenth century, and from these the Amish with their strict lifestyle and old traditions are descended.

The first Baptists were formed by the leadership of an independent preacher, John Smyth, in 1609, who had come under Mennonite influence on the continent. Some followers returned to England and opened the first Baptist church in London in 1612, led by Thomas Helwys.

How many sacraments?

Luther and the other Reformers argued that there were only two sacraments as Jesus had certainly instituted these – baptism and the eucharist. These are also known as 'sacraments of the Gospel'. This was not to deny the validity of things like marriage, ordination, anointing of the sick, confirmation and confession, but they were demoted from the level of sacraments. Some form of confirmation of belief and membership was retained, with or without bishops in attendance, and personal confession was encouraged for the quieting of conscience when it was felt necessary. The Council of Trent reaffirmed the traditional seven sacraments. The difference in understanding is about what defines a sacrament. If direct institution by Christ is the issue, then only baptism and the eucharist qualify. The Catholic position is that other things can be raised to sacraments either by his blessing (as marriage with his presence at Cana) or through the guidance of the Holy Spirit in the early church as with anointing of the sick (see James 5:14).

Sacraments were agreed by most of the Reformers (except Zwingli who probably saw them as symbols or tokens) to be efficacious means of grace. Cranmer held this line firmly, arguing that, 'Sacraments, ordained of Christ be not only badges or tokens of Christian men's profession, but rather they be a certain sure witness, and effectual signs of grace... ' (Article XXV). In his catechism, he defined a sacrament as 'an outward and visible sign of an inward and spiritual grace given unto us, ordained by Christ himself, as a means whereby we receive the same, and a pledge to assure us thereof.'

Orders

Clearly *sola scriptura* could not settle what ordination meant or what orders there should be in the church. We have glimpses of this in the New Testament, but no systematic exposition. The apostles were called by Christ; they appointed presbyters (elders) in the churches they founded. There were also deacons to serve in various ways. Later in the New Testament epistles the office of *episcopos* or bishop is mentioned as an overseer or chief presbyter. Was this office originally one and the same as that of the presbyter or is it different? The Reformers took different stances. Luther believed that bishops were useful as overseers and as a link with the early church. However, they were not essential and some Lutherans did not have them. Cranmer kept the threefold order of bishop, priest and deacon, seeing it as primitive and dating from the beginning of the church, but Calvin and Zwingli had only presbyters.

The ordinals of each church, the ordination rites, show that a Bible was given to the newly ordained minister/pastor/presbyter or priest. The Catholic Church, in contrast, gave a chalice signifying his power to celebrate the mass and offer that sacrifice. The Scriptures and the power to preach were primary for the Reformers.

Predestination

A secondary debate among the Reformers was the nature of predestination and election, that is, God's calling and choice of the redeemed person. Augustine of Hippo had written about this, urging care and caution, for God must always act justly. Passages which speak of God hardening Pharaoh's heart (see Romans 9:14–24) might only mean that Pharaoh's prior sins and attitude show that he was hard of heart and that God used this; God did not make him so deliberately like some sort of historical pawn. The elect were those who responded to the gospel but Augustine could never say that those who did not were predestined to damnation. We could not judge their eternal destiny or know the secrets of their hearts. Calvin, however, did go so far as this, and taught 'double predestination,' that is the belief that people are predestined either to heaven or to hell. This went hand in hand with Calvin's belief in the absolute sovereignty of God, i.e. that every event is foreordained, from the car crash to the epileptic fit. This was dangerously like saying that Christ did not die for all, a position already condemned by the Catholic Church. (In the past, it had been argued that as divine grace was irresistible, then those who refused it were already lost.)

In 1589 the Dutch Jacob Arminius tried to refute Catholic objections to predestination and failed. However, he found himself pitted against pure Calvinism. Arminius argued that God foresees who will be saved and that they are then the elect, but he desires that all should be saved. Such a departure from official Calvinism caused ructions and wars in his native Holland. The Calvinist/Arminian dispute has run right through the centre of Reformed belief ever since.

Reformation in England – establishment and dissent

The Reformation in England was never clear cut; it was a gradual affair with different groups pushing in different directions. There had been a desire for reform and interest in Luther's ideas by some during the early part of the reign of Henry VIII.

William Tyndale (c. 1494–1536), for example, translated the New Testament into English and had copies smuggled into England before his capture and condemnation. There was a brief return to Rome under the reign of Mary Tudor. Matters rested with the Elizabethan settlement in the latter part of the sixteenth century, as the Anglican Church saw itself as a middle way, or *via media*, between Geneva and Rome: the church in England was to be neither too Protestant nor too Catholic. This did stop Protestant dissenters or Catholics from trying to gather to practise their faith. Both sets of people were persecuted in what became effectively a police state. With the threat of invasion from Spain no dissent was tolerated. Catholics, especially priests, fared worse as many were executed for treason.

Edward VI

Edward's short reign (1547–53) was under the control of Lord Somerset as Protector of the Realm. Advances were made in the Reformed religion and Cranmer produced the first English Prayer Book in 1549. It felt Catholic in many ways, though its newness and simplicity caused rebellions in parts of the land where it was complained that it made religion sound like a Christmas game.

The second Prayer Book of 1552 went much further. John Knox was involved in its composition. The order of the mass, now 'the Lord's Supper', was changed further and tables were to be used. Eucharistic vestments were no more, only the surplice. Cranmer had produced an agreed Forty-Two Articles of religion that defined the stance of the Church of England by 1553 in a more Protestant direction, building upon Ten Articles produced under Henry in 1536. (Under Elizabeth these were whittled down to the familiar Thirty-Nine which are in the Book of Common Prayer. A committee of six had worked on these including Knox.)

Mary Tudor

Edward tried to create a Protestant succession by nominating Lady Jane Grey to succeed him in 1553, but she reigned for only a few months. The last days of Jane were chaotic, with one region after another coming over to Mary's cause. When she marched in triumph into London, people cheered her and statues of the old religion were placed in windows. The new faith was not yet in the hearts of the people and they welcomed the return of the old order. Many of the people lived quite happily with the old rhythms and devotions.

Mary sought to eradicate the Reformed faith and dissidents were arrested and often executed at the stake as heretics. Not all Mary's advisors agreed with these severe measures, such as the Spanish friars at court who pleaded that heretics be left alive so that they could be persuaded and repent. The records of the deaths of ordinary men and women, as well as leading churchmen like Cranmer, were written down a generation later in John Foxe's *Book of Martyrs*; they instilled a hatred of Catholicism for a long time to come.

Elizabeth I

The reign of Elizabeth I (1558–1603) saw the return of many Protestant exiles from Geneva where they had witnessed the government and structure of the Reformed Church under John Calvin. They returned to find an established church that was a middle way, a *via media*, between Rome and Geneva. They were 'Puritan' in belief, looking to the Scriptures only as the pure faith. Elizabeth refused to have a 'window to look into men's souls', as she put it, respecting freedom of beliefs, so long as they did not become a political threat. Later, in fact, Catholics did become such a threat. Attitudes worsened towards Catholics after the St Bartholomew's Day Massacre in Paris on 24 August 1572 when several thousands of Huguenots were killed over two days.[3] With the threat of Spanish invasion, anti-treason laws were passed against priests ordained abroad. Catholic priests travelled the land incognito, smuggled in from the continent, where English seminaries were established. The young men expected martyrdom; if caught, they faced the full penalty of the law, being hung, drawn and quartered in all its public barbarity, as happened to the Jesuit priest Edmund Campion (1540–81). Laity helping to hide them or to host a mass faced death by hanging or imprisonment.

At first, the returning Protestant exiles, known as Puritans, were tolerated; Elizabeth allowed debates and listened. Until the defeat of the Armada in 1588, she needed the loyalty of all her subjects; after that, however, things became worse for them. Some members of the Church of England, including its clergy, were Puritan in belief, and others formed independent congregations. Elizabeth forced such independents to emigrate to Holland where they found a freer Reformed Church and toleration.

Establishment and apostolic teaching

The 'Congregations', whether they were Puritan, some other form of Independents, or Baptists, saw the Church of England as only half Reformed, being infected with 'the dregs of popery'. What really united them was a hatred and fear of Rome. The Establishment answered back. It contained sensitive and learned theologians, and a number of devout men. Richard Hooker (c. 1554–1600) sprang to the defence of the Church of England in his *Ecclesiastical Polity*. He argued that the Bible was silent on many issues. It could not be used as a blueprint for church government as so much was not stated. The early church believed that it had followed apostolic teaching in some of its customs and these must, he claimed, have been passed on by a form of oral tradition. It was impossible to define exactly what was apostolic and what was man-made. This form of compromise became the established ecclesiology and a number of Anglican theologians flourished and developed it over the next few generations.

'No bishops; no king!'

When Elizabeth died childless in 1603, the only son of Mary Queen of Scots took the English throne. James I (1603–25) called an assembly of churchmen at Hampton Court to discuss matters of church polity and worship. James granted them only one request, for a standard and accurate English translation of Scripture, and the Authorized Version of the Bible was printed in 1611. The Puritans wanted to abolish bishops and have presbyters (elders or pastors) only. Traditionalists wanted to keep the bishops as a continuous link with the early Church (hence the episcopal or apostolic succession). James refused to budge on the issue of bishops, saying 'No bishops; no king!' and the Prayer Book remained unchanged.

Civil War and Cromwell

The tables turned in England with the outcome of the English Civil War (1642–51). Charles I was deposed and executed and Parliament abolished the Prayer Book and bishops, installing a Presbyterian Church in England, in fulfilment of a promise they had made to the Scots for their support in the fighting. Archbishop William Laud, an influential ritualist and supporter of the king, was executed. The 'Caroline Divines' were ritualistic churchmen who sought to study the early church fathers and use the Prayer Book with a more Catholic tone. Under their influence, stone altars had reappeared as well as decorative copes for the eucharist and they taught the doctrine of the real presence. Under Cromwell, they were removed from office and marginalized. Cromwell declared toleration for all believers except for Catholics and those who would install bishops as prelates of the realm again.

Quakers and Ranters

Various sects sprang up in such a fertile soil, such as the Levellers, the Seekers, the Ranters and the Muggletonians. The most successful were the Quakers, or the Society of Friends. The term 'Quaker' was an insult and a jibe, as many of their early followers shook and trembled when at worship and when hearing the Word preached. They exhibited the physical effects associated with revivalism and accounts of their founder, George Fox, suggest that they knew an experience of the Holy Spirit.

To the Quakers, God dwelt in the hearts of the believers and not in any buildings. This internalization led to a neglect of the sacraments ('having water sprinkled on a person makes them no Christian') and church order. Meetings were unstructured and any could speak as they felt moved. Women too were free to preach. The Friends were egalitarian and refused to doff their hats to the gentry. They also took a pacifist position, refusing to take up arms. Some of their behaviour became notorious for being wild and disorderly, including interrupting sermons, walking naked through the street and preaching personal visions, usually about judgment. The diarist Samuel Pepys recorded a quaint entry for 29 July 1667 when he was waiting for Charles II to appear to address a gathering:

> ... *a Quaker came naked through the hall, only very civilly tied about the privities to avoid scandal, and with a chafing-dish*

of fire and brimstone upon his head did pass through the hall,
crying, 'Repent, repent!'...[4]

The restoration of the monarchy

Another exodus from the Anglican clergy began with the Act of
Uniformity in 1662 upon the accession of Charles II to the throne,
after Cromwell's death. The Prayer Book was imposed upon all
parishes. Those who dissented faced exclusion from offices of
government and higher education or fines and imprisonment
or, worse, death. This was the era that saw men such as the
Presbyterian Richard Baxter, the Congregationalist John Owens
and the Independent hymn writer, Isaac Watts. By far the most
famous preacher of this time was John Bunyan of Bedford
(1628–88).

John Bunyan was born to poor parents, his father being a
brazier. He seems to have undertaken that trade and is described
in his youth as a 'tinker'. He fought on the parliamentarian
side in the Civil War and married in 1649. In 1653 he joined a
congregation of Independents and was recognized by them as
a preacher in 1657. He suffered under the measures of the Act
of Uniformity, spending most of the period 1660–72 in Bedford
gaol. But there he wrote, and devotional works such as *Grace
Abounding to the Chief of Sinners* poured from his pen, as well as
the classic allegorical tale *The Pilgrim's Progress*.

Bunyan was as typically anti-Catholic, writing a tract against
the pope which was published posthumously. However, he
displayed a sensitive, peace-loving spirit towards other believers.
Though he belonged to a Baptist church, he refused to let the
issue of water baptism break his fellowship with others: 'I will
not let Water Baptism be the rule, the door, the bolt, the bar, the
wall of division between the righteous and the righteous.'[5]

The Covenanters

The Scottish Covenant was an agreement to resist Charles I's attempts to impose bishops and the Prayer Book upon the Church of Scotland. During the Civil War the Scots sided with Cromwell, and when Charles II became king in 1660 he carried on the attempt to force episcopacy and the Prayer Book upon the Scottish church. The years 1661–85 were a time of trouble and severe persecution. Those who refused the new order formed themselves into 'conventicles', gatherings which met often, illegally, in the open air. They read their Bibles and worshipped. Covenanters were hunted down and killed on the spot after their numbers started to grow. Sometimes the Covenanters defended themselves and fought back, for instance at the battles of Drumclogg and Bothwell Bridge in 1679. Many were killed, imprisoned or transported. Various monuments mark the site of the martyrs or the battles to this day. England and Scotland demonstrate the trials and tribulations of the Reformation period, and the various stances the different Reformed groups could take.

Summing up

The Reformation saw much shedding of blood, mistrust and mutual hatred in the name of Christ. Christian hurt Christian, forming a terrible scar on church history. Calvin could sanction the burning of a Trinity-denying heretic; Mary Tudor burnt laymen at the stake; and Elizabeth had Catholic priests hung, drawn and quartered as traitors. This ancient shedding of blood places a cloud over the Reformation for all its insights, gifts and graces. A more peaceable closure to this chapter can be found in the words of Erasmus to Duke George of Saxony in 1524:

Well, let those who have no faith in saints' merits pray to the Father, Son and Holy Spirit, imitate Christ in their lives, and leave those alone who do believe in saints... Let men think as they please of purgatory, without quarrelling with others who do not think as they do... [6]

Timeline

1439	The Council of Florence released many Greek-speaking clerics into the West
1513–21	Pope Leo X raised taxes for St Peter's basilica by selling indulgencies
1517	Luther nailed the 95 Theses onto the cathedral door at Wittenberg
1520	Luther excommunicated
1521	Luther summoned to the Diet of Worms
1522	Zwingli began to form a Reformed Church in Zurich
1529	German princes issued their 'Protestation'; Luther met Zwingli at the Marburg Conference
1534	Henry VIII declared head of the church in England
1539	Formation of the Jesuits
1541	Calvin established himself in Geneva
1541	Colloquy of Regensburg between Melanchthon and Contarini
1545–58 1562–63	Councils of Trent
1549	First *Book of Common Prayer*
1552	Second *Book of Common Prayer*

1553–58	Persecutions under Mary Tudor
1572	St Bartholemew's massacre in Paris
1588	Defeat of the Spanish Armada
1611	Authorized Version of the Bible
1662	Act of Uniformity and the 1662 Prayer Book
1660–72	John Bunyan in Bedford gaol
1661–85	Severe persecution of the Covenanters in Scotland

At a glance

- Greek manuscripts and Greek-speaking Orthodox clerics helped to encourage a 'return to the sources', looking at the New Testament with fresh eyes.
- Rising literacy and the printing press helped to express new ideas and spread new writings.
- When Leo X sold indulgencies to help finance the rebuilding of St Peter's basilica, Luther nailed his 95 Theses to the door of Wittenberg Cathedral. By 1521, Luther was on trial, declaring, 'Here I stand; I can do no other.'
- Zwingli began reform of the church in Zurich and Calvin eventually settled in Geneva and ran a form of theocracy there.
- Henry VIII separated from the pope and declared himself to be the head of the church in England in the Act of Supremacy in 1534.
- The Counter Reformation aimed to convert Protestants back to the Catholic Church and to reform its behaviour. The Jesuits led the way, with notable individuals making their mark such as Philip Neri with the Oratory movement and Theresa of Avila with her reformed Carmelite order.

- A meeting of Catholics and Protestants at Regensburg found a large measure of agreement on justification, but the dialogue was rejected by both sides. The Council of Trent defined Catholic doctrine and practice, reaffirming transubstantiation and the seven sacraments. The Reformers held that there were only two sacraments, baptism and the eucharist. Some more radical leaders argued for believers' baptism, facing terrible persecution from fellow Protestants.
- Justification by faith, *sola fides*, separated the concept of justification from regeneration and inner sanctification. The Catholic Church held all three actions together in a unity.
- *Sola scriptura* and views on predestination were hallmarks of Reformed theology, but there were different views on a range of issues among them. Calvin taught double predestination and went further than any earlier writers.
- In England, the church became more Protestant under Edward VI, returned to the Catholic Church under Mary Tudor, and found a middle way, or *via media*, under Elizabeth I. Richard Hooker formulated the basics of Anglican theology as a church that is both Catholic and Reformed. James I kept episcopal succession in the face of Puritan demands, whilst Cromwell abolished bishops, for them only to be reinstated under Charles II with the return of the Prayer Book.
- Dissenters abounded in the post-Reformation Church in England, including Baptists and Congregationalists, with inspiration hymn writers including Isaac Watts and preachers such as John Bunyan.

Endnotes

1. Bamber Gascoigne, *The Christians*, Granada: London, 1978, pp. 169–70.
2. *Ibid.*

3. The Huguenots were not to gain toleration until the Edict of Nantes in 1598, enacted by the new king, Henry IV. He had been a Huguenot but had converted to accept the crown, with the comment 'Paris is well worth a mass'. This act was later revoked in 1685.

4. Bamber Gascoigne, *The Christians*, London: Granada, 1978, p. 228.

5. E. H. Broadbent, *The Pilgrim Church*, London: Pickering & Inglis, 1931, p. 254.

6. *Ibid.*, p. 124.

8. Into the Modern Age

The period from the seventeenth to the eighteenth century saw progress in science and philosophy that laid the foundations of the movement known as the Enlightenment. Many age-old assumptions were questioned, including the very foundations of the faith. The early Enlightenment thinkers were concerned to find a place for God but the movement became more radical and sceptical as time passed. This age also witnessed great revival movements in reaction, such as that under John Wesley. The philosophers turned to the head and the revivalists to the heart.

Enlightenment

The early seventeenth century saw the beginning of new philosophies and the rise of the scientific method. It was a time of great paradigm shifts. Up until then the scholastic system, based upon the thinkings of men such as Aquinas, had regulated knowledge and the study of the natural world. The early free thinkers were attempting not to deny God but to find clearer, and more testable ways of thinking about the universe rather than relying on ancient authorities.

Challenging the existing intellectual order could still result in being brought before the Inquisition in Rome, as happened to Galileo Galilei in the seventeenth century. He argued for heliocentrism, namely that the sun was at the centre of the universe and that the earth and other planets moved around it. In this he was following the older theories of Copernicus (1473–1543) who had been largely ignored. The Catholic Church at the time favoured Aristotle's belief in geocentrism – the view that the stars and the sun moved in a circular fashion around the central earth – which was thought to be the more likely plain meaning of Scripture. Galileo saw Scripture passages as poetic and thought they were not to be taken literally.

Galileo was condemned by the Inquisition in 1616 and forbidden to promote his theory, although he was allowed openly to discuss the two opposing views. Later, the new pope, Urban VIII, an old friend of Galileo's, regretted the earlier condemnation and sought his rehabilitation. He encouraged him to write his *Dialogue Concerning Two World Systems*, which set forth the arguments side by side. Unfortunately, the geocentrist views were expressed in a contradictory manner by their main protagonist, Simplicus, and some of the pope's views (which he had asked to be included) were placed upon the protagonist's lips, bringing ridicule. Fallen from favour, Galileo faced a heresy trial and was forced to recant his view that the earth moved. The *Dialogue* was prohibited from publication and he was placed under house arrest for the rest of his life. He is reputed to have whispered, 'But it still moves,' after his recantation, but this is not verified.

Galileo opened up the question of the interpretation of certain Scriptures, allowing them to be metaphorical. This meant that scientific observation did not come into conflict with faith. As he said in his *Dialogue*, 'The Bible teaches us how to go to heaven, not how the heavens go.'

René Descartes (1596–1650) wondered how to be certain about what he observed. Life could be a dream, an illusion, or a trick. After much reflection he concluded that the only thing he could be sure about was the existence of his very self. His self-awareness thought the thoughts in his head. This was the *cogito*, the thinking subject. He famously declared, '*cogito ergo sum*' ('I think, therefore I am'). From this premise he worked out a system of logic and observation that saw abstract ideas and constants behind reality and helped him form what we know as the scientific method of observation and testing. He caused an ideological revolution and fell foul of the church, living in more tolerant Holland for the last part of his life. Nevertheless, Descartes was a passionate believer, for the existence of God undergirded and confirmed the existence of the soul and of reality in his thought. The existence of God validated thought and all claims to truth, as it gave them a sure foundation. External reality depended upon him.

Descartes had opened a door for free thinking and others would take this path further, pushing God further and further away as the 'unmoved mover' who was necessary to start everything but had little or nothing to do with creation. Descartes held something like an immanent position, whereby God's abiding presence held reality in being. Still others wiped out any need for God at all, opting for a materialist position: only what could be observed with the senses was counted as real. Thus there were idealists, holding that God's order was implanted in the world and the mind, and empiricists, who looked to externals.

These early pioneers of the scientific method were deeply devout in their own way and their belief in a creator drove them to look for causal connections and rational theories. They expected to find order. In this they were following earlier philosophers such as Aristotle with his need for a 'first cause', and orthodox Christianity that rejected the radical dualism of Platonism and

Gnosticism. They challenged the Schoolmen, not in any attack on theism, but by refusing to believe that the ancients had classified all that there was to know and observe. There were still things to discover, and some views of the universe were outmoded with better theories and lenses for observation. The Scriptures could be interpreted more metaphorically and were concerned with faith, spirituality and morality rather than exact science.

By contrast, one of Descartes' contemporaries, who was equally a man of learning and the sciences, took a very different position. Blaise Pascal (1623–62) was a French mathematician and physicist who underwent an intense conversion experience, personal and mystical. He kept the testimony to this experience on parchment sewn into his coat:

> *From about half past ten in the evening until about half past midnight.*
> *Fire.*
> *God of Abraham, God of Isaac, God of Jacob, not of philosophers and scholars. Certainty, certainty, heartfelt, joy, peace.*
> *God of Jesus Christ...*
> *The world forgotten, and everything except God.*
> *Joy, joy, joy, tears of joy.*[1]

For Pascal the heart was the essential thing, for Descartes the head. Pascal joined the Jansenist movement, a reforming Catholic group who trusted in grace for salvation, despairing of their own efforts. These seventeenth-century thinkers typify the ebb and flow of faith in this age. One was putting more and more trust in logic and observation, the other in the emotions and the human spirit even though he was a well-educated intellectual of his day.

More radical thinkers

Descartes had worked from ideas in the mind outwards; others were to reverse this process. Ideas were formed by external stimuli. John Locke (1632–1704) developed a more sceptical approach than Descartes in his *Essay Concerning Human Understanding*. He sought truth by what was empirically observable and testable. He had room for God as the first cause, and some room for personal revelation, but God was more distant and impersonal. God could speak in the soul and in dreams and visions, but this was rare and not the rational norm of things. It was a dangerous, untestable enthusiasm. Locke taught the empirical way, rather than the idealist way.

Empiricism gave way to an atheistic scepticism as in David Hume (1711–76) or to a watered down faith as in deism where God was the absentee 'divine watchmaker'. Unitarianism also flourished; it saw Jesus as a teacher and rejected aspects of the New Testament such as miracles, the incarnation and the atonement. Dr Joseph Priestley (1733–1804) was a leading Unitarian thinker. People wanted no God, a distant God or a Jesus stripped of the miraculous. This was a new development, indeed.

Revival

By contrast, the eighteenth century was also a period of great revival in Europe, revival which spread quickly around the globe, with lasting social and political – as well as religious – implications.

George Whitefield (1714–70) was converted in 1735 and visited New England for six weeks of preaching. He had been involved with the Welsh revival (c. 1738–42) led by Howell Harris. Harris was a lay preacher working in North Wales from 1739. In 1752 he settled at Trevecca, which became a retreat and training centre for many in the revival.

Whitefield was a close friend of John (1703–91) and Charles (1707–88) Wesley. They had been members of a strict Holy Club at Oxford where their regular prayers and rules of life earned them the nickname of 'Methodists', for that was how they regulated their daily lives. In 1737, the Wesleys went on a mission to Georgia, America, for the Society for the Propagation of the Gospel, where they were frustrated with their own efforts and met Moravians, a brand of Christianity descended from the reformer Jan Hus. Their convinced, simple faith and inner peace in the centre of adversity impressed the Wesley brothers. When listening to a reading from Luther's *Preface to Romans* 24 May 1738 in Aldersgate Street, John experienced a deeper conversion; 'I felt my heart strangely warmed and I felt that I did trust in Christ, and Christ alone for my salvation.' He was to travel about 250,000 miles in his preaching trips, seeing hardened miners and labourers collapse in tears as they repented of their sins. However, John Wesley faced opposition. Although he was a convinced Anglican clergyman, he caused offence both by preaching outside his parish ('The world is my parish' he was to declare) and because of the enthusiasm occurring during his meetings. His followers were soon called Methodists after his old nickname. He resisted schism with the Church of England but his hand was forced when no bishop would agree to ordain clergy to lead missions in the America. He therefore ordained his own presbyters but felt the disunity was a deep wound until his dying day.

Nikolaus Ludwig von Zinzendorf (1700–60) was a Lutheran nobleman who as a young man founded the Community of the Grain of Mustard Seed with some friends to spread the gospel. He settled exiled Moravians on his estate and it became a refuge for many dissident Christians. Their different beliefs could have led to all sorts of wrangling, but a powerful experience of the

Holy Spirit at a communion service in 1727 produced much repentance and tears, forging them into a renewed community. The place was thereafter known as Herrnhut, the 'Hill of the Lord', and regular prayer meetings were held there for years. Von Zinzendorf became a bishop of the Moravians and travelled widely, using the term 'ecumenical' as we know it today for the first time.

This period in church history is referred to as 'the Great Awakening', a time of emotional revival during a sceptical age. This movement left behind many inspiring hymns and missionary societies, making a great impact upon the society of the day.

Mission and missionary societies

The fruit of the Great Awakening was the birth of various missionary and tract societies such as the Church Missionary Society, the London Missionary Society and the Baptist Missionary Society. In 1786, the Wesleyan Conference agreed to send a missionary to India. William Carey (1761–1834) was a Baptist minister who left his chapel in Leicester to become the first Protestant missionary to India. He was joined by Joshua Marsham and William Ward. He translated the Bible into several local dialects, founded mission schools and the Agricultural Society of India and was involved in the movement to abolish sati, the practice of burning widows on their husbands' deaths. He never left India. Carey was not the first missionary to India. Apart from the Mar Thoma Christians, who claimed their ancestry from the apostle Thomas, Jesuit missionaries had worked there to great effect, practising enculturation. Robert Nobili (1577–1656) had dressed as a Brahmin and even fed communion on a stick to the Dalits – the 'untouchables' with whom no other caste member would eat.

China had also had Jesuit missions many years but the first Protestant missionary, Robert Morrison (1782–1834), landed there in 1807. James Hudson Taylor (1832–1905) went on to form the China Inland Mission which sought to train Chinese converts for leadership so that Christianity was not seen as a foreign faith. This was a radical step at the time.

Another result of the Great Awakening was the birth of the Sunday school movement. Sunday schools were started by a Methodist, Hannah Ball (1734-1792), in 1769, and developed by a lay Anglican, Robert Raikes (1736–1811). The passion to convert and make disciples led to a concern for children and their basic Scriptural and moral education.

America

The American colonies had gradually built up an influx of immigrant Calvinists – English, Scottish and Irish Puritans, Independents and Anabaptists. The 'Pilgrim Fathers', for example, sailed from Holland and England on the *Mayflower* in 1620. These Calvinists had secretly left England for Amsterdam in 1608 where they co-existed with many other sects and groups (one contemporary comment was that Amsterdam was 'the fair of all sects'). Their community argued over doctrine and separated. Some went to Leiden in Holland, and others sought to go to America. There they would be the only sect and would therefore be able to create their ideal community. The *Mayflower* was only 100 feet (30 metres) long and had to house 102 pilgrims. They landed in Massachusetts in mid-November without shelter and were not able to secure a site for an encampment until the end of December. They struggled through, in great hardship and sickness until they had brought home the next harvest, an event celebrated each year in the American Thanksgiving. Thereafter they established New Plymouth with its simple wooden houses, church and stockade. Their story became famous by 1622, with the book *Mourt's Relation: A Journal of the Pilgrims at Plymouth.* Published in London, it told of their triumphs.

The Pilgrim Fathers saw themselves as the elect of the Lord and had no qualms about taking land from the native population. They brought European diseases such as smallpox with them and when this devastated the local native American Indian population, the governor wrote, 'God hath hereby cleared our title to this place.'

The moral code in Massachusetts was severe, regulating hairstyles, dress and personal behaviour. Lapses in morals would be punished and irreverent behaviour on the Sabbath might bring a whipping by Monday. Those who questioned the ministers were banished and a new community was founded on Rhode Island to allow greater toleration. Roger Williams (1603–83), a young minister, was to be sent back to England for his errant views, but he slipped away and settled in Rhode Island where he was joined by many others who subscribed to his views. He had been an independent preacher in London, an Anabaptist. His view was that people's moral failings were between themselves and God and should not be punished by others – this was referred to as 'soul-liberty'. Williams also disagreed with attitudes to taking the native American Indians' land. There was to be tolerance of different doctrines, as their code of laws stated, 'where all men may walk as their consciences persuade them, every man in the name of his God.' The American Baptists trace their roots back to Williams in Rhode Island.

Their tolerance was to be tested with the arrival of some Quakers, who reached the colony in 1656. Some were peaceful but others engaged in antisocial antics such as smashing bottles in the street, ranting in services, running naked and undressing in church 'under divine instruction'. This led to their being disciplined. They were banished but some kept on returning;

despite being whipped or mutilated, they returned again and again even when the sentence of death was passed. Williams resisted the violence shown to the Quakers but he repudiated their views, while maintaining their right to hold them.

The Quakers were eventually to find sanctuary in newly founded Pennsylvania, 'Penn's woods'. This was land which had been given to William Penn (1644–1718) by Charles II in repayment of an earlier loan owed to his father. Penn was a convert to the Quaker cause and he gladly welcomed his co-religionists to the new colony. He also preached tolerance to others, and when a woman was brought to him accused of witchcraft, ten years before the infamous Salem trials in Massachusetts, he asked her if she really rode a broom in the air. When she claimed that she did, he declared that there was no law against that and set her free!

Maryland, founded by Lord Baltimore in 1632 and originally an enclave for Catholics, also tried to practise toleration, although, once Puritans were in the majority, restraints were placed upon Catholics and Anglicans.

Other arrivals in America included the Huguenots who had fled persecution when Louis XIV revoked the Edict of Nantes in 1685. France lost about 400,000 industrious, skilled workers and many formed the community of New Rochelle in 1688. Also escaping persecution were the Dutch Reformed émigrés and Lutherans who arrived in large numbers. Their religion tended to be Congregational, rather than Episcopal, with close co-operation across denominational boundaries as the settlements became established. In 1648 this agreement was expressed in the Cambridge Platform.

The first-generation settlers might have had commercial hopes but they were also fired by an evangelistic zeal and the hope of a godly society. The second generation was more compromised and religion became more formal and moralistic.

Whereas membership of a church had been based upon evidence of commitment and the new birth, now anyone could attend who was not notorious. The Half Way Covenant, for example, allowed children of uncommitted parents to be baptized. This would previously have been unthinkable.

The Lutherans brought pietism, a movement that looked to the Lord in the heart, and to spiritual renewal, through thinkers such as von Zinzendorf. This appeal to the heart brought new light to the lifeless religion that had settled into most of the states. In 1690 the population of the colonies was about 250,000 and mostly British. After the arrival of the Huguenots, the Dutch and the German Lutherans, the situation changed. By the middle of the eighteenth century there were about 200,000 Germans alone in North America. Various ministers and pastors lit the fire of the Great Awakening there, including the Dutch Reformed minister Theodore Frelinghuysen in New Jersey. Jonathan Edwards (1703–1758) was said to be the initiator in Northampton, Massachusetts. In 1734 he reported, 'The Spirit of God began extraordinarily to set in.' Many were converted – 'souls did as it were come by floods to Jesus Christ' – and when Whitefield visited in 1740 the crowds were so great that he had to preach in the open air. In the next few years about 150 churches had been affected as far apart as New York, New Jersey, Pennsylvania, Maryland and Virginia. Whitefield sought to rouse the ministers for 'The reason why congregations have been so dead is because dead men preach to them.' As clergy caught the fire, so did their people.

When the Declaration of Independence was signed in 1776, there were strong spiritual roots that helped the formation of the new nation. The founding fathers of the constitution were versed in the Scriptures and part of a heritage of faith. This is summed up by the story told of the young soldier George Washington (1732–99) when he was a redcoat lieutenant-colonel. He was shot at many times by the American Indians, yet he was not hit. A chief declared that this man was under the protection of the Great Spirit. Later, Washington found four bullet holes in his coat, yet the bullets had not gone through to him. This became the stuff of legend but the belief in providence and divine guidance was deep in the hearts of the drafters of the Declaration of Independence.

Christian sects

During the nineteenth century a number of heterodox Christian sects arose in the USA such as Christian Science, the Christadelphians, the Seventh Day Adventists, the Church of the Latter Day Saints and the Jehovah's Witnesses. This was in an age when some were looking for a new beginning, a new order in the New World, questioning many accepted precepts and expecting an imminent return of Christ. The tradition of toleration and wandering preachers helped to give birth to new traditions and outlooks.

Mary Baker Eddy (1821–1910) began the Christian Science movement with a strong belief in healing. She taught that the mind has more reality than matter and can influence the body. Sickness is therefore an illusion, and Christ's technique of spiritual healing can be released by studying the Scriptures, as she explained in *Science and Health* in 1875.

The Christadelphians were founded by John Thomas (1805–71) in 1848. He wanted to return to the simple beliefs and lifestyle of the first Christians and he adopted the term 'Christadelphian', 'Christ's brethren', for 'Christian' had too much to do with institutional religion and apostasy. His teachings were apocalyptic, looking for the return of Christ to begin a new kingdom in Jerusalem. Christadelphians reject the doctrine of the Trinity.

The Seventh Day Adventists derived from the Adventists, various apocalyptic groups in the USA who expected Christ to return in 1844. One group came to hold the Jewish Sabbath as binding for Christians and avoided alcohol and tobacco, also encouraging abstinence from tea, coffee and meat. Their doctrine was otherwise orthodox and they remain Trinitarian.

The Church of the Latter Day Saints, also known as the Mormons, was founded in New York by Joseph Smith (1805–44) in 1830. He claimed to have had a revelation of the angel Moroni and golden tablets that held the text of the Book of Mormon. This was about the teaching of the risen Christ to the lost tribes of Israel in America. Both the Bible and the Book of Mormon are therefore sacred Scriptures. In 1843 he claimed to have been told by God that his followers could practise polygamy. This caused controversy and Smith was killed by a mob in 1844. Brigham Young (1801–77) took over the movement, relocating their headquarters to Salt Lake City, Utah in 1847. The federal government tried to stop cases of polygamy until in 1890 the president of the church advised its members to conform to the law. The Mormons are strongly adventist, looking forward to the return of Christ, and they only accept a modified form of the Trinity whereby there are three deities.

The Jehovah's Witnesses were founded by C. T. Russell (1852–1916) as the 'International Bible Students'. According to their beliefs, only members of this group were the true elect of Jehovah and would reign in the coming messianic kingdom on a renewed earth. The saints and apostles of the Bible were the literal 144,000 of the redeemed who would reign in heaven (Revelation 14:1). Jehovah's Witnesses have their own translation of the Bible, the New World translation, which changes some texts to make small but significant differences in doctrine. Russell's successor, J. F. Rutherford (1869–1941), developed the view that Witnesses must pledge no allegiance to any nation for they belong to a 'theocratic Kingdom', and this made many countries suppress the movement during 1939–45. Witnesses reject the Trinity, claiming that Jesus was an archangel, a view that is not unlike that of the Arians in the fourth century. They have indulged in speculations about the end of the world, once claiming that Christ would return in 1914. They now teach that he came into a new level of his spiritual kingdom in that year, as a stage preparing for the imminent end.

Social reform and abolition of slavery

The Awakening set in motion a number of reform movements besides missionary endeavours. These arose from the premise that this world was important as well as the next, and that it mattered how people lived. The Evangelicals were a group of Anglicans in the early nineteenth century who shunned the non-conformism of the Methodists and the strict Calvinism of other independent groups. They remained loyal Anglicans and their ranks contained the influential Clapham sect, whose members included such men as Lord Shaftesbury (1801–85) and William Wilberforce (1759–1833), who did much to change their world. Shaftesbury campaigned about the conditions for children in the mines, and Wilberforce initially pressed for a change in morals, seeing a decline in cock-fighting and bear baiting, before turning his attention to the emancipation of slaves. He campaigned constantly for the abolition of the slave trade, raising public consciousness of the conditions in which these men and women were kept. In 1807 the trade was abolished, and slavery itself was prohibited in 1833. Wilberforce also campaigned for the 'white slaves', the urban poor who worked long hours for a pittance in the factories.

Such men cared much but feared revolution and too much democracy. They defended the social order against radical campaigners and presented a benevolent approach, refusing to let the poor help themselves but stressing that the rich had a duty to help them. This was against the background of fears about the French Revolution.

Nineteenth-century revivals

Revival movements continued apace in the nineteenth century; examples include the movement under the ministry of Dwight Moody (1837–99) in the USA or the rise of the Salvation Army under Methodist minister William Booth (1829–1912) in England, with his motto 'Blood and Fire'. Booth combined fiery preaching and appeals to conversion with direct, social action among the slums and the problems of drink. The Brethren withdrew from Anglicanism and non-conformism, fearing that belief was not radical enough or pure enough. Some withdrew into closed communities, and others, the 'Open Brethren', often became involved in missionary and charitable work. One of these was Dr Barnardo who started his homes for orphans in 1870. After the death of 'Carrots', a youth who was turned away when the home was full, Barnardo adopted the policy of never refusing a child admission.

The Eastern churches

After the fall of Constantinople in 1453, many Orthodox Christians were under Muslim domination. Russia was the main exception, with Moscow being proclaimed as a third Rome after the end of the Byzantine empire. Muslim rulers were usually tolerant but forbade proselytizing by the Christian communities. The churches became more guarded and protective of their traditions. Though the Orthodox never underwent anything akin to the church-splitting Reformation in the West, they were inward-looking in some senses and unable always to engage with their culture or enter a free and creative dialogue. The liturgy, mainly the fourth-century rite of St John Chrysostom, was preserved intact, avoiding any changes, even minor ones. The liturgy became the depository of much Orthodox tradition, faith and identity.

It would be wrong, however, to see Orthodoxy as stagnant, afraid and moribund. That would be to do it a great disservice. There was a spiritual renewal movement that looked to the interiority of the heart, a form of mystical pietism, that was, in a way, an Eastern form of those sweeping the West in the Age of Enlightenment.

The hesychast movement, exemplified in the teachings of St Gregory Palamas (c. 1296–1359) stressed the indwelling Spirit. This movement is named after the Greek *hesychia*, meaning quiet or silence. It derived from the monastic rhythm of prayer at first but then spread in forms of lay devotion. It is based upon inner recollection and the repetition of a prayer, usually the Jesus Prayer. Such repeated phrases are known as monology. The believer cultivated a sense of abandonment to God, of inner calm and of a sense of the Holy Spirit's presence.

Ascetic, hesychast texts were collected together in the *Philokalia* by Nikomedos of the Holy Mountain, and by Makarios of Corinth in the eighteenth century. This collection was translated into Russian by Theophan the Recluse in the nineteenth century, inspiring a golden age of mystical prayer in the Russian church. The anonymous work *The Way of a Pilgrim* popularized the practice of the Jesus Prayer in daily life for ordinary people.

This brief piece of advice from the *Philokalia* captures the heart and vision of the whole enterprise:

Let us therefore imitate our fathers and like them let us seek
the treasure within our hearts. And when we have found it,
let us hold fast to it with all our might, both cultivating it

*and guarding it (cf. Genesis 2:15), for this is what we were
commanded to do from the beginning.*[2]

Such Christian mysticism did not claim direct union with God as
did some forms of non-Christian traditions. The believer merely
touched the hem of Christ's robes, to use a gospel analogy
(see Mark 5:28). The Spirit of God was experienced, or God
was encountered through his energies but not in his essence.
Orthodox writers speak of a continual transformation by the fire
of the Spirit that is endless, or of entering the cloud of God's glory,
like Moses on Mount Sinai, but walking in a certain darkness of
unknowing while enjoying the divine presence. It is humble, in
progress and a lifelong journey of discipleship.

The transformation and glorification of the body by one so
open to God could cause visions of the divine light and also have
people seeing the saints shining with light like Moses of old, as
in the case of St Seraphim of Sarov (1759–1833). He was one of
the noted *starets* or elders in the Russian church in the nineteenth
century whom people sought for prayer, healings and counsel.
He had supernatural insights into people's lives, healing miracles
attached to him and he was once seen as transfigured by the
divine light. A Russian, Nicholas Motovilov, came to him for
counsel and recorded a conversation and experience they had
one day in mid-winter in the forest:

*Then Father Seraphim took me firmly by the shoulders and said:
'My son, we are both at this moment in the Spirit of God. Why
don't you look at me?'*
*'I cannot look, Father,' I replied, 'because your eyes are flashing
like lightning. Your face has become bigger than the sun, and it
hurts my eyes to look at you.'*
*'Don't be afraid,' he said. 'At this very moment you yourself
have become as bright as I am. You yourself are now in the*

fullness of the Spirit of God; otherwise you would not be able to see me as you do...'
'What do you feel?' Father Seraphim asked me. 'An immeasurable well-being,' I said.
'But what sort of well-being? How exactly do you feel well?'
'I feel such a calm,' I answered, 'such peace in my soul that no words can express it.'[3]

The tradition of the holy elder was captured by Dostoevsky in his *The Brothers Karamazov* with the elder Zosima. An example of this spirituality can be seen at work on the eve of the Bolshevik revolution in the ministry of John of Krondstat (1829–1908) who attracted crowds to his liturgies and for confession.

Liberal Protestantism

Responses to the Enlightenment took different forms. Some were revivalist as seen above. Others were more accommodating and sceptical, such as deism. A new, intellectual approach held to God as a first cause, and a guarantor of morality, but little else. Immanuel Kant (1724–1804), for example, tended towards an ethical theism. Religious doctrines were really of value only if they influenced our behaviour. He had no time for the doctrine of the Trinity as this had nothing to with morality. This type of thought denied any real place for divine revelation.

Other reactions were more experiential or emotive but lacked the clear orthodoxy of those involved in the revival movements. Søren Kierkegaard (1813–55) steered away from intellectual debate and historical controversy and into the heart. Faith was an action, a passionate thing, not just intellectual assent. Faith was a choice, a leap in the dark; Christianity had to be lived not argued. Yet, was it any more than a personal choice? There was a cutting loose from objective foundations for faith. Or, again, Jean-

Jacques Rousseau (1712–78) sought faith and purpose in nature and its beauty. He had been a Calvinist, then a Catholic and a Calvinist again before leaving established religion behind. It was with nature that he could commune with his maker. These were some typical reactions to the challenge of the Enlightenment and its separation of faith and reason.

The lives of Jesus and biblical criticism

With so much rejection of traditional dogma and religion, what did people make of the figure of Jesus? The eighteenth and nineteenth centuries saw attempts to rethink the story of Jesus. Post-Enlightenment thinking stressed reason. The supernatural was to be questioned if not jettisoned. Writers tried to rescue the real, historical Jesus from the sceptics and ended up with a passionate teacher, a freedom fighter, a social reformer, a visionary, a dreamer, or an inspiring ethical teacher. If God remained in the story (and he did not always do so) Jesus taught simply the 'fatherhood of God and the brotherhood of humanity'. Some key authors here were Herman Reimarus (1694–1768) and J. E. Renan (1823–92). Reimarus wrote about natural religion based upon morality and reason (1744–67), and Renan wrote a revisionist *Life of Jesus* (1863).

Another approach was to speak about the power of myth as inspired symbols and poetry rather than being embarrassed by it. D. F. Strauss (1808–1874), for example, wrote his *Life of Jesus Critically Examined* (1835–36) to hold out a teacher of divine love and great moral truths. He saw all miracles and supernatural elements as mythical, not fabrications to be rubbished but moral and spiritual truths dressed up. The supernatural elements in the gospel were coded insights – miracles were about the joy of new beginnings; atonement was about the possibility of reconciliation.

Albert Schweitzer (1875–1965) studied all the published liberal lives of Jesus and summarized his findings in *Quest of the Historical Jesus* (1905). His conclusion was that there was something strange, alien to us culturally in the teaching of Jesus. He was an apocalyptic prophet ('He comes to us as One unknown... ') but for all the uncertainties, there is an abiding truth:

> *Jesus means something to our world because a mighty spiritual force streams forth from Him and flows through our time also. This fact can neither be shaken nor confirmed by any historical discovery. It is the solid foundation of Christianity.*[4]

The values, the spirituality, the impact of the Man still resonate even if we can debate the veracity of some historical details in the Gospels.

The modernists

The end of the nineteenth century also saw a reassertion of papal authority with the definition of papal infallibility at the First Vatican Council (Vatican I) in 1869. This meant that in very specific circumstances, with the consent of the worldwide bishops, the pope could speak with infallible authority on matters of dispute. The pope had recently lost the Papal States, and Leo IX asserted his role by saying, 'Tradition? I am tradition!' 1854 had seen the definition of the immaculate conception declared as dogma. This is the belief that Mary was preserved from the stain of original sin to allow her to carry Jesus in her womb. Again, revivalism had a distinct shape in the Catholic world, where the healing shrine of Lourdes started with visions of the Virgin to a peasant girl, Bernardette Soubirous, in 1858.

A similar approach to the Liberal Protestants was taken by the Catholic theologian, Alfred Loisy (1857–1940). He saw truth and revelation as abiding in the ongoing faith of the church and not in exact historical studies. The impact of Jesus and the faith it inspired was what counted. He went further, however, arguing that the faith has to develop and be reshaped by the present. He also was sceptical about finding the actual teaching of Jesus in the Gospels. He and his fellow 'modernists' as they came to be known, were condemned by Pope Pius X in 1901.

Dealing with Darwin

Another ideological revolution was to explode in the nineteenth century. Charles Darwin (1809–82) published *The Origin of Species* in 1859 followed by *The Descent of Man*. This sparked off fierce controversy although Darwin was no committed atheist and always held an agnostic position about a creator. As author Charles Kingsley (1819–75) commented: 'They have to choose between the absolute empire of accident, and a living, immanent, ever-working God.' The Baptist preacher C. H. Spurgeon (1834–92) denounced the theory as a 'monstrous error'. Bishop Samuel Wilberforce's (1805–73) public debate with Thomas Huxley (1825–95) resulted in a triumph for the scientist who appeared as a humble seeker after truth. Gradually, theologians cleverly integrated evolutionary theory. The Genesis accounts were seen by many as picturesque myths conveying profound truths about the nature of the world and of humanity. Rome also accepted this position in the early twentieth century, though creationism is a large and influential movement still. All Christians believe in the creation; but creationists take the biblical account literally, not figuratively.

The Oxford Movement

A need for sure faith and revelation that could be believed in, as well as a love of the visual and the ritualistic, produced a reforming movement in the Church of England in the latter part of the nineteenth century. This also echoed the romanticism of the period in the arts. The Oxford Movement sought to call the Church of England back to its apostolic roots and the teachings of the early fathers. John Keble (1792–1866) attacked the government for suppressing Irish bishoprics in 1833, claiming that the state had no such authority. Men such as Frederick William Faber (1814–63), John Henry Newman (1801–90) and Edward Bouverie Pusey (1800–82) influenced the movement. A series of *Tracts for the Times* were published and Newman eventually attempted to prove that the Thirty-Nine Articles were compatible with Catholic doctrine as found in the Council of Trent in Tract 90. When the bishops attacked this he became disillusioned and became a Roman Catholic in 1845, eventually rising to cardinal.

Later Oxford Movement priests developed a greater enthusiasm for ritual and the grandeur of the mass. Vestments were reintroduced, as were altar crosses, candles, reservation of the sacrament, processions and sacramental confession. John Mason Neale (1818–66) was one of the first to reintroduce eucharistic vestments and he translated many medieval and Eastern hymns into English encouraging a new body of devotion. Many of these early Anglo-Catholics were slum priests, running mission churches in London or the south coast and showing great love and pastoral care of their flocks. Some were imprisoned for periods, becoming the victims of lawsuits and ecclesiastical courts over their use of ritual that was not prescribed by the Prayer Book.

Reactions

There were two responses to the liberal musings. One was to reaffirm orthodoxy, as happened with the rejection of Loisy (see above) by the Catholic Church. On the Protestant side this can be seen in the release of the *Fundamentals*, a twelve-part series of booklets, in 1909. These stressed the need to maintain orthodox faith such as belief in the virgin birth, the bodily resurrection and the miracles. (The term 'fundamentalism' derives from these but the authors were not talking about a particular, literalistic idea of the inspiration of Scripture, just about its key doctrines.) An appeal to the heart, to the feelings, also ran through the eighteenth and nineteenth centuries. What was perhaps lacking was a more careful intellectualism that admired faith and tradition, had a humble admiration for the mystical, but would grapple realistically with new issues of the day. This period saw no one like Aquinas or the other great medieval theologians. The great thinkers of this period were more sceptical and philosophical.

Timeline

1633	Galileo forced by the Inquisition to recant
1650	Death of Descartes
1690	Publication of John Locke's *An Essay Concerning Human Understanding*
1727	Holy Spirit revival at Herrnhut
1735	Whitefield converted
1738	Wesley's conversion at Aldersgate Street
1740	Height of the Great Awakening in the American colonies
1769	Birth of Sunday Schools
1833	Start of the Oxford Movement
1833	Death of Seraphim of Sarov
1835–36	Strauss's *The Life of Jesus Critically Examined* released
1854	Doctrine of the immaculate conception proclaimed

1859	Publication of Darwin's *The Origin of Species*
1869	Definition by the First Vatican Council (Vatican I) of papal infallibility
1901	Condemnation of the Catholic modernists

At a glance

● Thinkers such as Galileo and Descartes championed the scientific method of observation and experimentation rather than relying on ancient authorities such as the Schoolmen.

● Locke laid the foundations of further scepticism with his belief in reason and a marginalizing of revelation. Hume and others were even more sceptical.

● The Great Awakening in America and Britain was a revivalist appeal to experience and the heart, which was also found in the pietist spirituality of Lutherans and Zinzendorf.

● Whitefield and the Wesleys were powerful preachers of their time.

● Various missionary societies and activity resulted from revivalism, such as the Church Missionary Society and also the pioneering work of Hudson Taylor in China.

● The United States had a spiritual mixture of various immigrant groups who brought different denominations with their different kinds of spirituality. A broad consensus and co-operation resulted as seen in the Cambridge Platform. Heterodox sects also formed such as the Church of the Latter Day Saints and the Jehovah's Witnesses.

● In England, the evangelical Clapham Sect campaigned for social reform – leading figures included Shaftesbury in the mines and Wilberforce against the slave trade.

● The Eastern churches were largely under Muslim rule but they developed a rich devotional life of interior prayer using

the Jesus Prayer. Holy monks and elders were a strong
example to their people and were sought for counsel.

● Liberal *Lives of Jesus* began to appear, trying to rehabilitate
Jesus from the supernaturalism of the Gospels.

● The Catholic Church had its own revival movement
centred on the shrine at Lourdes, and reasserted orthodoxy
with the definition of the immaculate conception and also
the teachings of the First Vatican Council. The Catholic
modernists tried to adapt the insights of the Liberal
Protestants, but were later condemned.

● In the debate with Darwinism, various churchmen gradually
accepted that the theory of evolution was compatible with
faith and more symbolic, poetic interpretations of the book of
Genesis gained ground.

● The Oxford Movement tried to restore aspects of Catholic
theology and ritual to the Church of England, though some of
its leaders such as Newman became Roman Catholics.

Endnotes

1. Blaise Pascal, from Don Cupitt, *The Sea of Faith*, London:
BBC, 1984, p. 52-53.

2. Niphoros the Monk, 'On Watchfulness and the Guarding of the
Heart', quoted in G. E. H. Palmer, Philip Sherrard and Kalistos
Ware (trans. and eds.), *The Philokalia Vol. 4*, London: Faber and
Faber, 1995, p. 195.

3. Fedotov, *A Treasury of Russian Spirituality*, quoted in Timothy
Ware, *The Orthodox Church*, London: Pelican, 1963, pp. 131–32.

4. Albert Schweitzer, *The Quest of the Historical Jesus*, London:
SCM Press, 1954, p. 397.

9. The Twentieth Century

The nineteenth and twentieth centuries saw rapid technological progress in a relatively short time span. Mass media and transport revolutionized society with the invention of the telephone, the wireless, the cinema, steam ships, railways, the automobile and the aeroplane. This was the world of modernity – the world of new inventions. 'Modernism' was a philosophical movement that celebrated progress. It was dealt a harsh blow by the two world wars that ravaged the twentieth century. It was a time of increasing scepticism about faith, with Emil Durkheim arguing that God was just a projection of our ideals, Karl Marx treating religion as the opium of the people, and, in the early twentieth century, Sigmund Freud piloting psychoanalysis. Revival and renewal movements flourished, however, countering this scepticism and beginning to give hope after the devastation of war. Biblical criticism was accepted but handled carefully, with a more orthodox approach appearing among some theologians and scholars.

Revival and renewal

Wales began a revival in 1904, which lasted for two years.

Pubs closed and rugby matches had to be cancelled. People were falling in the streets under conviction of sin, weeping. Across the world in Kansas, some of Charles Parham's students began speaking in tongues, such as Agnes Ozman. They tried to organize missionaries according to their tongue but soon realized that this was probably heavenly language to be used for worship. In Azusa Street, Los Angeles, Walter Seymour, a one-eyed, shy black preacher, knelt in a garage where people had gathered to pray for revival. The charismatic gifts, such as speaking in tongues and prophecy (see 1 Corinthians 12:4–11), were manifest and crowds started to gather. They sat on the dusty floor, oblivious to their surroundings, and were made up of many denominations and ethnic groups. Many of their leaders rejected this new spirituality. Perhaps they feared emotionalism and enthusiasm; perhaps they were dispensationalists (evangelicals who believe that the charismatic gifts ended with the age of the first apostles); perhaps they were challenged by the inter-racial harmony demonstrated. Thus people were forced to form new denominations, some named after the day of Pentecost in Acts 2 in the New Testament when the Holy Spirit was poured out: the Pentecostal churches. Many taught that the believer needed a 'second blessing' of baptism in the Holy Spirit, evidenced by the gift of tongues.

Pentecostal experience and charismatic gifts began to appear in mainline denominations in the 1960s and the 'second blessing' theology was soon modified into a more general 'renewal in the Spirit' which sounded less elitist. Moreover speaking in tongues was seen not as a necessary sign of renewal, but as a gift that is open to all. The renewal came into the Catholic Church in 1967 at Duquesne University in Pittsburgh, USA. Professors and students met together to read *The Cross and the Switchblade* by David Wilkerson, a Pentecostal preacher who went to the gangs of New York. The renewal soon spread to Notre Dame University in Indiana. Renewal spread throughout the Catholic Church so that it has been estimated that about 100 million Catholics in 120 countries are involved. David du Plessis, a Pentecostal leader, held ongoing dialogue with charismatic Catholics between 1972 and 1982. Charismatic Catholics gathered in Rome in the 1970s to meet with Pope Paul VI who gave them his blessing. Footage of this meeting shows them standing in applause as he is carried in – the last of the popes to do this – as thousands of people sing in tongues.

A lasting effect of charismatic renewal has been a greater ecumenical openness as barriers are broken down by a common experience of the Spirit. This spiritual renewal movement birthed new songs and styles of worship that have crossed denominational boundaries and have encouraged ecumenism. Ecumenical dialogue and co-operation was, perhaps, the ecclesiastical hallmark of the twentieth century. Worship took on more spontaneity, short, simpler Scripture songs, modern instruments and more lay participation.

The Bolshevik Revolution

The Bolshevik victory in October 1917 and the rise of Marxism–Leninism in Russia heralded an era of persecution for the Orthodox Church there and for other believers. The Orthodox were in a state of effective siege until about 1988 when the Russian church celebrated its millennium. Some have noted an earlier prophecy from Archpriest Avvakum 300 years earlier: 'Satan has obtained our radiant Russia from God, that she may become red with the blood of martyrs.'

Though freedom of religious belief was promised under the new constitution, propaganda and evangelism were not permitted. Church influence was removed from education and all property was confiscated. No pastoral visits could be made to hospitals or study groups. Gatherings were allowed for worship, but priests and bishops had to have state permission to minister, and their every word and movement was monitored by the secret police. There was a militant atheism in power that sought to suppress religion. As Stalin put it, 'The Party cannot be neutral towards religion.' It was hoped that with materialistic education and curtailment of church activities, religion would gradually die out. Under Stalin, numerous clergy and religious figures were sent to the gulags. At least 130 bishops were executed and there are no accurate lists for priests. It is thought that this would run to the tens of thousands.

Stalin relaxed matters somewhat after 1943 and the war with Hitler; some buildings were reopened and a few seminaries were allowed. There were still no other freedoms and any teaching had to be done in the sermons during the liturgy each Sunday. The Soviet Christians thus developed the tradition of long services with lengthy or multiple sermons. Laity were not exempt and other denominations were rounded up too. Believers might find that their progress in employment or in further education was curtailed because of their religious faith. Evangelical groups such as the Baptists were particular targets during the Soviet era as they were zealous for the faith and sought to make converts. Stories of those tortured and imprisoned made their way to the West, especially when some were released and relocated, such as Pastor Richard Wurmbrand of Romania. His experiences were written in *Tortured for Christ*. The author Alexandr Solzhenitsyn captured the trials of life for a lay believer in the gulags in *A Day in the Life of Ivan Denisovich*.

There were attempts at resistance in the late 1960s and early 1970s with *samizdat* literature being circulated. These were cheaply produced books and pamphlets on home printing presses. Gradually, stories and conditions became known in Europe through agencies such as the Christian Committee for the Defence of Believer's Rights, working with the Helsinki Monitoring group, and Keston College in England. Official meetings and speakers at the World Council of Churches claimed that there was freedom in the USSR and that no criticisms were heard. Matters eased only with Gorbachev's policies of *glasnost* and *perestroika* when he came to power in 1985. By 1992, the communist era was over and the Soviet Union no longer existed.

Ecumenism

This century saw unprecedented moves towards Christian unity. Earlier revivals had crossed certain Protestant denominations and forged co-operation between missionary societies. The twentieth century was to go much further, partly as a response to two horrific world wars. In 1910, Protestant co-operation was overseen by the International Missionary Council, which evolved into the Life and Work movement in 1925 looking at social concerns. The Faith and Order movement followed in 1927 at Lausanne, examining matters of doctrine. Both met again in 1937 in Edinburgh and Oxford respectively. These emerged into the World Council of Churches in 1948, after the Second World War. The experience of the world wars was a huge impetus for the churches to work together.

The First World War resulted in much heart-searching and desire for peace between Christians. The eumenical patriarch (the patriarch of Constantinople, the leading Orthodox bishop) issued such a call in 1920 that created fruitful relations between Orthodox and Anglicans, leading to the formation of the joint Society of St Alban and St Sergius whose members met for conferences and published papers together.

The Malines Conversations ran from 1921–25 in Belgium. These were the result of contacts between Lord Halifax, a leading

Anglo-Catholic, and Cardinal Mercier. The Conversations took place with the full support of Rome and Canterbury. The real presence was agreed, as well as an unbloody, mystical sacrifice in the eucharist, the need for bishops and the supremacy of the pope. However, other sections of the Church of England were not enthusiastic. In fact, they were completely antagonistic. The report on the Malines Conversations was published just before the vote was to be taken in Parliament in 1928 on proposed revisions to the Book of Common Prayer. These revisions leaned more in a Catholic direction and the vote was lost. Protestant sections of the Anglican Church feared 'popery'.

Anglicans and Methodists became involved in dialogue which began in 1950 and ended in 1972. In 1946 Archbishop Fisher invited the free churches to accept episcopacy and to seek reunion with Canterbury. Only the Methodists were interested. The newly formed General Synod in 1970 with its houses of laity, clergy and bishops had to have a two-thirds majority of votes cast in each and this failed. The failure was over how to reconcile Methodist orders: some wanted full episcopal ordination, some wanted immediate acceptance and some wanted a service of reconciliation that was ambiguous – did it propose to bless Methodist ministers or to top up whatever was missing in their ordination?

Meanwhile the English Presbyterians and the Congregationalists agreed on a merger and they formed the United Reformed Church in 1972, after about forty years of discussions. Earlier, a radical unity move had been made in India where the Church of South India was set up in 1947 including Methodists, Presbyterians, Congregationalists and Anglicans. Again there had been years of planning, beginning in 1919. The churches simply united without pressing episcopal ordination of non-conformist ministers. This caused alarm in parts of the worldwide Anglican communion, which saw it as a form of unacceptable compromise.

World Council of Churches

The first meeting of the World Council of Churches took place in Amsterdam in 1948 and was attended by 147 denominations. It held people to a minimal confession of faith in the 'Lord Jesus Christ as God and Saviour'. Pope Pius XII praised the gathering and encouraged its work but would not let Catholics join, although he did lift a ban on discussions with non-Catholics.

The Delhi meeting in 1961 had a confession that extended to 'one God, Father, Son and Holy Spirit'. The Orthodox had now joined (hence the clear Trinitarian formula), as had the Pentecostals under David du Plessis. There was a split in 1968 in Sweden between liberals and conservatives over mission; some thought this was social concern, others thought it should be primarily about conversion.

Taizé

Roger Schutz was a Calvinist pastor. Fresh from seminary, he set up a Reformed monastic community in the small village of Taizé in France with a few friends. This was not far from Cluny, the site of a famous medieval monastic community, now in ruins. During the war, they sheltered Jewish children but had to flee from the Gestapo. Returning after the war, they found a German prisoner-of-war camp nearby and they reached out to the prisoners, befriending them. Their vision of reconciliation started to grow and with it the conviction that there would be no peace in Europe until there was peace between the churches. The community has grown and hosts large gatherings, mainly of youth, each summer for retreat, Bible study and fellowship. There are many nationalities and languages spoken. This one, relatively small experimental community has had far-reaching effects. As well as its call to work together, its simple chants in

Latin or many different languages have spread around different churches throughout the world.

Billy Graham and international evangelism

Billy Graham (b. 1918) has probably preached to more people worldwide than any Christian who has ever lived. It was reckoned by 1993 that more than 2.5 million people had come forward at his crusades to make a decision for Christ. His style is to preach a gospel message and then to make an appeal to the crowds. A person comes to a counsellor and makes a profession of faith in Jesus Christ as their personal Lord and saviour. The following testimony of a young person at such a rally is typical:

I listened to the preaching and didn't feel anything, really. Then when Billy Graham asked people to step forward the air was electric. I felt the hairs on the back of my neck standing up and I felt compelled to get up out of my seat. I struggled against this at first as I was with some friends, but I had to give in.

Graham was converted by an evangelistic campaign in 1934. The USA has had travelling preachers and crusades for years, a reminder of the days of the Great Awakening. A tent came to town, people were leafleted and invited to the meetings. Popular, rousing hymns were followed by a gospel message with an appeal to be saved or to commit your life to Christ. These were from the free churches but often operated in a non-denominational capacity. The converts were the responsibility of the local churches.

Graham married Ruth Bell, the daughter of Chinese missionaries, in 1943, formed the Billy Graham Evangelistic Association, and began a radio programme, *The Hour of Decision*, in 1950. He started to travel the world, holding campaigns in major cities. His personal charisma and use of mass media have allowed him to capture such an audience, as well as being the confidant of various US Presidents, though his friendship with Richard Nixon brought him much criticism. Other US evangelists have launched similar ministries with global offices and travel to hold campaigns, but they are following in the pioneering footsteps of Graham's organization, which used twentieth-century technology to take the message further afield. The world of satellite TV has since opened up a whole new arena for later generations of evangelists.

Vatican II

When Pope John XXIII was elected he was in his late seventies. Some no doubt thought he would be a safe, caretaker pope after the long pontificate of Pius XII. He stunned many by calling a second Vatican Council in 1962. There were 2,500 delegates who participated and non-Catholic observers were invited, which would have been unthinkable at Vatican I. The theologians Karl Rahner (1904–1984) and Hans Küng (1928–) were among the advisers. This had strong ecumenical implications as it affirmed other Christians. They were seen not as full churches but as 'ecclesial communities', gatherings of Christians who did not all have the necessary hierarchy or sacraments in Rome's view. Still, they were brothers and sisters and worshippers of the same Lord, described as 'separated brethren'. Prior to this, they had tended to be classed as schismatics and heretics. A common baptism was affirmed, and converts to the Catholic Church no longer had to be rebaptized. Important moves were made by Pope Paul VI (who closed the council after the death of John XXIII) to heal the breach with the Orthodox as he met the ecumenical patriarch, who, in turn, lifted the anathemas that had been pronounced against the pope years before in 1054.

Other important changes were that the liturgy of the mass was to be in the vernacular and reading the Bible was encouraged, including non-Catholic editions. Pulpit and altar were to be of the same height where possible in churches to stress that Word and sacrament were equally important.

The Jews were acknowledged as part of the ongoing people of God. Any sense of their guilt for the death of Christ was removed. Pope John XXIII had personally insisted on dropping the term 'perfidious Jews' from the old Good Friday liturgy. The gifts and wisdom of Judaism were now clearly appreciated.

This council shook up the Catholic Church and opened it to modern society. A decree was issued on religious freedom and on social concern. Other religions were also treated with respect and it was stated that anything that was true and good within them was not to be rejected. This decree has been the strongest affirmation of world religions by a Christian church yet, while acknowledging that Christ is unique.

A key development was a refining of the position that there is no salvation outside the church. The Catholic Church was now seen to subsist, in all its essentials, in the Roman Catholic Church. Other gatherings of Christians had some of the marks of the church, the Orthodox especially. The Catholic Church was the fullness of the church and the recognition of the validity of baptism outside this church allowed a far greater ecumenism whereby others were already joined in an imperfect communion with the Catholic Church by virtue of that baptism.

With other faiths, the door was opened to recognize that there were those who stood outside the church who knew something of the revelation of God in their hearts or consciences, however imperfectly, and there were ways that God came to individual non-Christians: to quote the Council, God came, 'in ways known to himself'. These were not equal ways of salvation, but God's activity was not absent from them. Theologians such as

Karl Rahner spoke of there being 'anonymous Christians' in other religions, and some went further, denying the need for missionary work apart from social help. The Vatican issued a clarification in 2000, *Dominus Iesus*, and dismissed overly liberal attitudes, restating the uniqueness of Jesus and the need for evangelization.

There were sweeping changes and much enthusiasm and expectation, but Catholic doctrine as such was unaltered.

Dialogues

The fruit of such ecumenical encounters can be seen in various official dialogues such as the Lutheran/Roman Catholic meetings which found a substantial agreement on justification by faith; the Anglican/Roman Catholic (ARCIC) discussions which began with the Windsor statement on Eucharist and Ministry in 1980, and the Lima text, *Baptism, Eucharist and Ministry*, in 1982. This was organized by the World Council of Churches and had 100 theologians looking at these areas. The main proposals were:
1. There should be mutual recognition of each other's baptism.
2. The eucharist should be the main Sunday celebration.
3. Lay ministry should be encouraged alongside ordained ministry. There was a great openness to the role of bishops as they linked the present churches to the early church.

Justification by faith

In 1983 the US Lutheran–Roman Catholic series of dialogues produced a substantial report entitled 'Justification by Faith. They concluded that the twin processes of acceptance because of Christ's death and infusion of grace through the Holy Spirit were complementary though not identical. The real difference was over which was the prior, or the main or 'formal', cause. The

Reformers had classed the acceptance as justification with the infusion as regeneration/sanctification. The Catholic position had always classed the whole saving event as justification, stressing that this was an ongoing experience throughout life in a growth in holiness. This classification was side-stepped in the dialogue as both sides affirmed the acceptance and the infusion as working together in harmony. They were essential parts of one event. Anglican dialogues have also seen the distinction as irrelevant. The action of God is all of a piece and is to be celebrated.

The eucharist

Much fruitful dialogue has been held over the eucharist and the idea of memorial has been used in a new, dynamic manner. In the Bible, *anamnesis*, usually translated as 'memory' or 'memorial', means a living reminder, bringing the past into the present. At the Passover, Jews are in the presence of the living God who set the slaves free. At the eucharist, believers are in the presence of the living Christ who died for them, and he is the Lamb who was slain. It is not just bringing to mind a historical memory, but standing in the midst of all its power and reality. The Lima text, a consultation between members of various denominations, said this:

> *The eucharist is the memorial of the crucified and risen Christ, i.e. the living and effective sign of his sacrifice, accomplished once and for us all on the cross and still operative on behalf of all mankind.*

This is the fruit of praying and dialoguing together. Much the same is affirmed in ARCIC and the Lutheran–Roman Catholic dialogue. Note the sixteenth-century Council of Trent's statement on the memorial:

Therefore our Saviour, when about to depart from this world to the Father, instituted this sacrament, in which He poured forth, as it were, the riches of His divine love towards men, making a remembrance of his wonderful works... [1]

The great difference was in the uncompromising belief in the real presence through the miracle of transubstantiation; the Council of Trent had rejected any idea of a mere symbol or sign, or a force (probably in response to Calvin's concept of dynamism). Many of the Reformers feared that too real an association with the sacrament of the body and blood might open the door to notions of re-sacrifice. There were common misunderstandings about this in the medieval period. 'The sacrifice of the mass' is for the Catholic Church primarily the 'once for all' historical event on Calvary, and secondarily the offering of prayers and praise by the people. Christ's sacrifice is sacramentally represented, and its memorial is alive and active, full of spiritual power to convict, atone, forgive and heal. On an earthly altar or holy table, in sacramental bread and wine, this offering, once offered on the cross, is present and proclaimed at one and the same time as the presence of Jesus as the Lamb who was slain, pleading for humanity in heaven. The sacrifice of the mass is propitiatory because the cross is re-presented, and the cross was propitiatory.

More dialogue is necessary about the sacrifice of the eucharist; however, there is greater agreement on the real presence among many Christians today even if this is far from settled.

Theological struggles

The Liberal Protestantism of the nineteenth century still held sway in much of the twentieth century, fuelled by the critiques of religion put forward by Marx (1818–83) and Freud (1856–1939). Both saw religious faith as irrational and illusory. Religion represented symbolic hopes or repressed guilt. Scepticism among theologians had its contenders. The Catholic convert G. K.Chesterton (1874–1936) was bemused, 'I grew up in a world where Protestants who just proved that Catholics do not believe the Bible were excitedly discovering that they did not believe it themselves.'

Rudolf Bultmann (1884–1976) played a different hand with his programme of demythologizing. He might have been certain of only one truth in the Gospels, that Jesus died on a cross, but he believed in the living reality of the God who was revealed in Jesus and the impact of that revelation in society. It could not be grounded in much history, but something was there to respond to. He drew a division between the Jesus of history and the Christ of faith, a division that has influenced many New Testament theologians since. He believed that there was something of substance to the Christ of faith, and how little history there was in the Gospels did not matter. (The apostle Paul probably would not have been very impressed with Bultmann's scepticism about the history on which his faith was based.) Some later scholars (for example, the scholars of the US-based Jesus Seminar) have been more sceptical, seeing the Christ of faith as a creation of the early church and a radically different figure from Jesus, whom they seek to reinvent as a wandering preacher and healer.

Bultmann's programme of demythologizing substituted depth psychology and existential philosophy for the supernatural. His programme dealt with fear, alienation, reconciliation and authentic living instead. It was a developed form of liberal Protestantism whereby we are fundamentally able to better ourselves with some self-realization. He poured scorn on any literal, supernatural views in *Kerygma and Myth*:

> *It is impossible to use electric light and the wireless and to avail ourselves of modern medical and surgical discoveries*

*and at the same time to believe in the New Testament world of
demons and spirits.*

This was, it is interesting to point out, written at the time that the
saintly Padre Pio (1887–1968) claimed the stigmata in Italy and
ministered to many of the Catholic faithful, who believed that
his prayers healed and that he had supernatural insight into their
souls. The age of belief in the supernatural is not actually over; it
has not been eradicated by the Enlightenment.

Bultmann's was not the only influential voice in early
twentieth-century theology. A more careful, but critical
orthodoxy was espoused by others. The Swiss theologian Karl
Barth (1886–1968) published his commentary on Romans in 1919.
He followed aspects of biblical criticism, but stressed the central
truths. Romans spoke of the saving word and saving grace. God
speaks into our world and our needs and is based upon real and
objective revelation in the life of Jesus. This undercut the optimism
of Liberal Protestantism, and was timely as it came after the evils
of the First World War. It has been said that this work 'fell like
a bomb on the playground of the theologians'. Barth's believing
but critical position became known as neo-orthodoxy.

Barth stressed on the need for grace and the objectivity of the
incarnation, atonement and resurrection. His neo-orthodoxy
influenced future generations of scholars who thought that there
was a substantial historicity to the Gospels, even if some things
were the work of later redactors.

The Catholic Church gradually adapted to critical biblical
studies and took a careful but open approach, so long as
key doctrines were not rejected. Even before Vatican II such
methodology was encouraged and the Genesis stories, for
example, were seen as symbolic. Later, post-war German
theologians have followed neo-orthodoxy, arguing for objective
revelation and some history in the Gospels; such theologians

include Jürgen Moltmann with his *Crucified God* or Wolfhart Pannenberg with his *Jesus, God and Man*.

Dietrich Bonhoeffer

Dietrich Bonhoeffer (1906–45), a German Lutheran, was involved with the Confessing Church set up by the Barmen Declaration in 1934. This rejected the view that German Christians had to venerate nationalism and accept anti-Semitism. Leading pastors and theologians signed this, including Karl Barth and the outspoken pastor Martin Niemoller (1892–1984) who spent some years in a concentration camp. The declaration shook up German Lutheranism with its usual neutrality to state politics; supporting Nazism was a bridge too far for some. Bonhoeffer set up a Confessing seminary at Finkenwalde in 1935 which the Gestapo closed in 1937. He left for the USA but finally returned, and was arrested in 1943 for links with a conspiracy to assassinate Hitler. He was executed in 1945 just before the end of the war.

Bonhoeffer's unfinished collection, *Letters and Papers from Prison*, throws out suggestions, images and ideas for a theology that he did not have the time to refine. Here he speaks of humanity as 'come of age' and not needing God. God is squeezed out in weakness. He states a need for a 'religionless Christianity' and these views have been debated and claimed for various other, extreme positions. Probably all that he meant was a rejection of pomp, pride and ceremony and a false pietism that sought to ignore social and human needs. A careful reading of his work suggests that he meant that in a technological, scientific, confident society, people can choose to get along without God in everyday life. God is pushed out, but in his weakness we see the cross. How true this must have seemed in the triumphalism of the Nazi Reich. God was pushed out on Calvary and he is no different now. He is a still, small voice which whispers in hearts nonetheless, seeking trust and discipleship for its own worth. Such a path has to be earthed and ordinary and cannot hide behind the externals of organized religion alone.

Bonhoeffer spoke of the pressing need for a Christology 'from below' where we start with Jesus as 'the man for others' and work towards his deity. Christianity needed radical discipleship that avoided cheap grace and made changes in society and in the ways in which people behaved towards each other. He wrote in the furnace of Nazi persecution.

Talk of religionless Christianity and Jesus as the 'man for others' was taken up by avant garde theologians during the radicalism of the 1960s – for example the death of God movement led by Thomas J. J. Altizer (1927–) believed that God is a projection of human ideals and an outmoded belief, but that Jesus has value as a moral teacher and someone who helps us point beyond ourselves. Others sought to substitute God language for the depth language of human experience – for instance Paul Tillich (1886–1965) who coined the term 'the ground of our being' for deity – though they leave open the door for transcendence and mystery. Bonhoeffer might have had some sympathy for Tillich as he spoke of God as 'the Beyond in the midst' but he would have been appalled by Altizer.

The Civil Rights Movement

Christian witness and conviction led to the formation of the US Civil Rights movement in the 1950s and 60s. Martin Luther King (1929–68) was a key player. He was ordained a Baptist minister in 1947 and qualified with a Doctor of Philosophy degree from Harvard. When serving as pastor of a Baptist church in Montgomery, Alabama, he became involved in the National Association of Coloured People, campaigning for justice, being only too aware of discrimination from his own youth. In 1955 he became president of the Montgomery Improvement Association which led a boycott of the buses by all blacks for 382 days. This was over the arrest of a black woman, Rosa Parkes, who had refused to give up her seat to a white person.

The Civil Rights movement evolved as people wanted to speak out more. Many urged violent uprising but King refused and instead followed a careful route of non-violence. He was inspired by the Indian leader Gandhi, who, in turn, sought to follow Jesus' words from Matthew 5:38-39 in the Sermon on the Mount:

> *You have heard it was said, 'Eye for eye, and tooth for tooth.'*
> *But I tell you, Do not resist an evil person. If someone strikes*
> *you on the right cheek, turn to him the other also...*

King was ridiculed, arrested, bombed, sent abusing calls and letters, and eventually assassinated in 1968 when greeting the crowd from his hotel balcony in Memphis, Tennessee. In 1962, he met President Kennedy, and one year later, he led a march of 250,000 people (including 60,000 whites) to Washington to support the Civil Rights Bill being debated by Congress. This was passed in 1964, the same year that King was awarded the Nobel Peace Prize. He donated the $54,000 to the Civil Rights movement.

One of his famous speeches included these words:

> *I have the audacity to believe that peoples everywhere can have*
> *three meals a day for their bodies, education and culture for*
> *their minds, and dignity, equality and freedom for their spirits.*
> *I believe that what self-centred men have torn down, other-*
> *centred men can build up. I still believe that one day mankind*
> *will bow before the altars of God and be crowned triumphant*
> *over war and bloodshed... I still believe that we shall overcome.*

Liberation theology

South of the equator, another movement was developing in Latin America in the 1960s. The 1950s had seen demoralization about the effects of aid to help the economy and intellectuals began to turn to the example of Marxist Cuba as a better way forward. Many priests became influenced by this thinking and entered into a dialogue with Marxism. They were concerned with social justice and one priest, Father Camilo Torres, declared 'The Catholic who is not a revolutionary is living in mortal sin.' He was shot in 1966.

The general thrust of liberation theology is an emphasis on *praxis* (action) rather than dogma or *kerygma* (preaching). How people live and how we respond to social injustice is paramount. It came from South America – where leading liberation theologians include Leonardo Boff of Brazil, Gustavo Gutierrez of Peru, Juan Secundo of Uruguay and José Miranda of Mexico – and the context of life in the developing world was formative. Gutierrez seeks to find points where the Bible and church tradition respond to, or speak into, social concerns. He was inspired by the story of the exodus as a biblical event of liberation where slaves are set free and oppressors overthrown. These theologians speak of a bias for the poor and call out for radical reforms.

They work in countries where the church has a shortage of priests and many religious and lay catechists run parish groups. These often form base communities where people can have fellowship, read the Bible and support one another, for example by marching in protest about a lack of sanitation in a village. The church and the clergy are often close to the lot of the very poor and hence their concern. Not all clerics have espoused Marxism, however. Dom Helder Camara (1909–99), the former Archbishop of Olinda and Recife in Brazil, spoke up for the poor but did not embrace Marxism. He criticized the USA and Europe for being 'enclosed and imprisoned in their egoism' and he advocated radical protest, but always of a non-violent type. He once commented, 'When I give food to the poor, they call me a saint. When I ask why the poor have no food, they call me a communist.'

The work of some liberation theologians was curtailed in the 1980s by Pope John Paul II (1920–2005) when concern was expressed about their Marxism, links with politics and violence and questions about doctrine. This was not to disparage concern for the poor nor to denigrate the hard work done by many priests among such communities. Rather, this action sought to restore a certain balance as the Vatican saw it.

The rise of Christian charities

Charity has always been a Christian virtue; it is a translation of the Greek word *agapē* for a costly love. Individuals and monastic orders, special confraternities or trusts have exercised charity towards various groups. The nineteenth century heralded the rise of the International Red Cross, based upon the vision of one man, Henry Dunant (1828–1910) after the battle of Solferino in 1859. Dunant was born in Geneva and worked successfully in commerce. His memoirs of the battle were published in *A Memory of Solferino*, the last part of which appealed to the nations in all Christian conscience to form a relief movement, with the necessary training, to aid the wounded. This resulted in the Geneva Convention in 1864 and international fundraising and co-operation in the treatment of war wounded that founded the Red Cross movement. This was achieved without the means of mass communications available in the twentieth century; when these came into existence, various aid agencies were to be created.

The twentieth century saw the rise of international charities with Christian foundations. These are organizations with paid staff, large administrative needs and professional experts as well as a round of advertising and fundraising activities. The beginnings were often very modest. For example, OXFAM began as the Oxford Committee for Famine Relief concerned about the plight of families in former Nazi-occupied countries such as Greece. Now OXFAM works worldwide with thirteen confederate organizations in over 100 countries.

Christian Aid also began after the Second World War. This was the result of an appeal by British and Irish church leaders to aid the situation of European refugees. The movement was called 'Christian Reconstruction in Europe' at first, and later the 'Department of Inter-Church Aid and Refugee Service'. It became, simply, Christian Aid in the 1950s under a new, visionary president who started to ask questions about the real, long term causes of poverty. Janet Lacey looked beyond Europe to the world situation and launched the first Christian Aid week in 1957. Christian Aid also helped to create VSO, 'Voluntary Services Overseas'. By 2006, a record £93 million was raised.

CAFOD, the Catholic Agency for Overseas Development, began in 1960 when the National Board of Catholic Women organized a Family Fast Day for refugees. In 1962, the Catholic Bishops of England and Wales officially set up CAFOD with the aim of providing a focus for all the small-scale charitable efforts which were already taking place.

These and many other groups, set up simply for a particular appeal, have become streamlined and international. They are concerned with being proactive rather than reactive, looking at questions of debt cancellation, fair trade, and promoting local projects to create wealth in developing nations. They developed in this way because of the mass media possibilities in the post-war society. Largely as a result of the world wars, the twentieth century has left the creative legacy of ecumenism, dialogue and charitable work.

Timeline

1904	Welsh revival
1906	Azusa Street revival
1917	Bolshevik revolution in Russia
1918	Karl Barth's commentary on Romans
1920	Ecumenical patriarch issued a call to unity
1921–25	Malines Conversations between Roman Catholics and some Anglicans
1925	Life and Work movement founded
1927	Faith and Order movement founded
1928	Proposed changes to the Book of Common Prayer rejected
1934	Barmen Declaration founded the Confessing Church in Germany
1947	Church of South India established
1948	World Council of Churches founded
1962–65	Second Vatican Council (Vatican II)
1963	Civil Rights march led by Martin Luther King to Washington DC
1967	Charismatic renewal entered the Roman Catholic Church at Duquesne and Notre Dame universities in the USA
1972	Failure of unity talks between Anglicans and Methodists; formation of the United Reformed Church
1982	Lima text, Baptism, Eucharist and Ministry

At a glance

- Scepticism continued in the early part of the twentieth century with Marxism and psychoanalysis. Two world wars increased this for some but caused a revival of faith for others, and new attempts at co-operation.

- Revival broke out in Wales and in Los Angeles in the early 1900s, birthing the Pentecostal movement and, later, charismatic renewal in the mainline denominations. This also took root in the Catholic Church by the late 1960s.

- The creation of the USSR started seventy years of persecution for the Russian church and for other believers.

- Ecumenism developed after the First World War, between Orthodox and Anglicans and various initiatives began which resulted in the creation of the World Council of Churches in 1948. Early conversations between Anglicans and Catholics were fruitless, but, since the Vatican Council reforms, high level dialogues have been held with Lutherans and Anglicans, showing much convergence in doctrine.

- Mass media saw the rise of international evangelists such as Billy Graham, who tried to appeal across the denominations.

- Vatican II allowed liturgy in the vernacular and recognized the validity of baptism in other denominations. There was a new openness to ecumenism and social justice. The Jews were no longer blamed for the death of Christ.

- Dialogue about the eucharist has begun to break down old barriers of mutual condemnation and misunderstanding, to the point of a high convergence in the multi-denominational Lima text. Much has been made of the concept of *anamnesis*, memorial. This has also informed Roman Catholic dialogue with Lutherans and Anglicans.

- Liberal Protestantism continued, including the revisionism of Bultmann's demythologizing programme. However,

Barth led a neo-orthodox movement that took seriously the objectivity of revelation and humanity's need for grace.

- Bonhoeffer struggled with the place of religion and faith in the modern world as he worked against the Nazi threat, calling for a humble, weak, servant model of church that was involved and relevant. His ideas have, however, sometimes been hijacked by more avant garde theologians.
- Martin Luther King and the Civil Rights movement campaigned for justice for blacks in the USA in the 1960s.
- International charities were created after the Second World War or in the early 1960s to respond to refugee crises or famine. These came from Christian roots with church backing, often ecumenical.

Endnotes

1. Council of Trent, Thirteenth Session, II, quoted in Rev H. J. Schroeder, OP, (trans.), *The Canons and Decrees of the Council of Trent*, Illinois: Tan, 1978, p. 78.

10. Emergent, Mission-shaped, Fresh and New

The twenty-first century has seen a desire to find new, fresh expressions of church whether evangelical, charismatic or Catholic. There is an attempt to return to the sources, to the life and flexibility of the first churches, and to be 'incarnational'. This means finding people and reaching out to them where they are, from the Christian doctrine of God becoming man to meet his creation on its own level. There are creative programmes of evangelism, gatherings for worship in cafes and dynamic new movements that gather people together with vows and commitments. Some movements are theologically conservative but there are also contemporary theological debates and explorations about the authority of Scripture, the role of women or homosexual rights.

In the developing world, Christianity is becoming stronger than in the secular and affluent West because there is more openness to spirituality. The churches also suffer persecution in certain areas and can produce a vibrant witness to the faith that impacts on parts of the developed world. It is often said that Christianity in the developing world might overtake the role and witness of that in the West.

Postmodernism

The twenty-first century is often described as 'postmodern'. There are many definitions of postmodernism (in fact, that is one of its defining characteristics), but it is basically a post-Second World War outlook and philosophical movement that has reacted against the structures and certainties of modernism. Birthed in an age of mass media, rapid communication and many voices, images and styles, it is decentred. Absolute truth is rejected and people find themselves swimming in a stream of ever-moving ideas. Truth is a project, unfinished and in progess. Human beings cannot know everything or have an objective, God's-eye view. We have to live with contingency and humble limitations. We have many little, local stories and suspect the credentials of big stories, or metanarratives as they are described.

The philosophy of postmodernism has been forged largely by French thinkers and émigrés, sometimes in the Jewish tradition, though many of the seminal thinkers who are seen to have formed postmodernism would not have called themselves by this label. They might have used others, such as 'phenomenologists' or 'post-structuralists'. Emmanuel Levinas (1906–95), for example, an orthodox Jew, spoke of the value of the 'other', the value of the person, and the mystery of being. He was rooted in the values of Torah. Jacques Derrida (1930–2004) was an Algerian Jew who was fascinated by the notion of God and faith but who said 'I rightly pass for an atheist'. Some postmodern philosophers are very sceptical, avoiding any sense of objective truth, such as Michel Foucault (1926–84) and Jean Baudrillard (1929–2007). The latter famously argued that the Persian Gulf War had not really happened: it was a media stunt, a selective programme of images and claims on our television screens.

This sceptical, fluid view of life might be thought to be challenging to the gospel and some postmodern thinkers are indeed atheistic. However, the rediscovery of intuition and poetry, mystery and narrative over against discursive reason (working everything out in systems) has much to offer spiritual renewal and discipleship. The head is turning to the heart. How do people do 'church' in this context, a context of rapid change, of various styles and subcultures, of scepticism and indifference to the gospel? There are many people who are searching and dabble in spirituality in an uncommitted, 'New Age' manner, picking and choosing from world faiths, ancient rites and mantras. They are far from being materialistic and there is a growing interest in mystical or pagan forms of spirituality.

In response to the above, some Christians practise a committed, vibrant discipleship with traditional worship and values; others are more experimental.

The emergent church

This is a US-based phenomenon where people are emerging from one position into another. They stress that this is not a movement but a conversation, an unfinished, learn-as-you-go-along process. Some emergent churches are huge, such as Mars Hill Bible Church led by Rob and Kirsten Bell with 10,000 worshippers in a converted mall. One of Rob Bell's sayings is 'Weak is the new strong'. This emphasizes the church's provisional, searching nature – it is not about having answers. There is a desire to be relevant to youth culture and the media, ever moving and changing their style.

Another tenet is that small can be beautiful. Other emergent groups are much smaller, provisional and intimate such as

Solomon's Portico with its homely sofas and mix of ancient and modern styles – it looks like a coffee shop. Spencer Burke runs such a small gathering from his garage, having left a more conventional megachurch (US megachurches grew out of the charismatic movement and large, evangelistic rallies, numbering thousands). He felt increasingly alienated by its structures, impersonal rhythms and management procedures.

These leaders of emerging church are influenced by culture not only in style, but also in philosophy. Postmodernism defines their way. They are also influenced by the seminal emergent thinker Brian McClaren. In his book *A New Kind of Christian* there is a fictional dialogue between failed pastor Dan Poole and the enigmatic schoolteacher nicknamed Neo. It is not Jesus or the faith but the worldview that is changed and challenged. Neo explains that modernism was about objectivity, analysis and control. Postmodernity is more open and flexible.

The issue is about belonging before believing, or discipleship rather than belief. Lifestyle is witness, not claiming absolute truth. Grace and a redeemed community are emphasized, not a theology of judgment and hell. And no one has all the answers.

Many of these leaders and thinkers are former traditional evangelicals who have thought 'out of the box' and felt constrained. Kirsten Bell felt that 'Life in the church had become too small'. In the emerging church there is less room for systematic theology. 'We want to embrace mystery rather than conquer it.' The Bible is still important but more ambiguous, not all understandable and often open to interpretation. This might be about styles of worship, or morals (is homosexuality really unscriptural?) or questions of objectivity – what was the feeding of the 5,000 really all about? Perhaps it should be seen as a symbolic story where Jesus teaches the value of sharing with one another. Thus some emergent Christians are liberal evangelicals.

There is a rethinking of salvation as holistic and not just a personal experience or eternal life insurance policy, as Brian McClaren stated: 'What does it mean to be "saved"? When I read the Bible, I don't see it meaning "I'm going to heaven after I die". Before modern evangelicalism nobody accepted Jesus as their personal saviour, or walked down an aisle or said a sinner's prayer.'

Emergent church is seeking, experimenting, engaging with culture. It is creative, imaginative and tries to be relevant. However, it is also reacting against a narrow form of belief and worship and critics sometimes see it as over-reacting. Experimental services, modern chants, video clips and ambient music in informal contexts might be creative and valuable, but critics argue that the emergent people have had too narrow a background and have misrepresented evangelicalism. They are drawing false antitheses between truth and experience, evangelism and discipleship, believing and belonging. Such critics see emergent thinking as reactionary and not as open or hopeful or gospel as it claims to be. They also ignore more traditional church groups who can still bring in the crowds as well as youth. The 'old, old story' still has pulling power.

Fresh Expressions and Mission-shaped Church

The UK has seen the effect of emergent church, but more on style and evangelism than theology with the exception of the theology of the post-evangelical movement which is prevalent at the Christian Arts festival, Greenbelt, or the more controversial writings of Steve Chalke, a Baptist pastor and director of the Oasis trust charity. In the UK, these are people who have been very conservative evangelicals but who are now freer thinking and are reacting to aspects of their subculture. Mainline evangelicals have embraced the styles but kept the doctrines.

Multi-media youth or student services and local, small and

imaginative outreach are growing. The Church of England issued a report 'Mission-shaped Church' about church planting programmes and, as Bishop Graham Cray commented, it is 'a great moment of missionary opportunity'. The report explores the changes in society, the increased mobility and fragmentation of communities. There are subcultures and networks and a less cohesive society. It encourages special styles and approaches for different groups, whether youth groups or professionals. Thus there can be a Goth eucharist in a Cambridge city-centre church that is near a Goth night club. Another group has opened a worship meeting in a school hall, with bouncy castles and doughnuts to attract children and families. Asian believers host their own evening gatherings with food and worship in a congenial style. These new initiatives are focused on particular groups such as youth, skateboarders, the coffee culture, or ethnic communities.

These initiatives are known as 'Fresh Expressions' of church. Fresh Expressions are working beyond the parish or denominational structure but it is not clear at this stage how they relate to existing structures of church. How are people introduced to the wider tradition of the church from their experimental, relaxed, modern worship? These are new questions for a new century and sometimes can be points of tension between the new groups and traditional congregations.

New ecclesial movements

The Roman Catholic Church has numerous movements that are renewing its life and mission. These are usually a mixture of lay, religious and clerical. They might organize themselves like societies or religious orders. They have rules of life and their own discipline and vision. They are started by one or two individuals with a particular vision or charism (a particular gift or insight). One priest at the Vatican has claimed that about thirty new applications per week are received for approval. These movements might be small or large and all have very different characteristics. Some are overtly charismatic and some are more contemplative.

One of the earliest to be formed, during the mid-twentieth century, was Focalare. This focused on community and living out the life of the gospel. The stress is on unity around the hearth (*focalare*). It began during the Second World War. In 1943, in Trent, Italy, the bombs were falling as a young woman, Chiara Lubich, was sheltering. She took a book of the Gospels and the words came alive. She could not tear herself from the farewell discourses in John, especially the phrase, 'May they all be one'. She gathered some friends and they prayed at the altar for guidance. They took the maxim, 'Love your neighbour as yourself' and went out seeing who might be in need of help – the old woman struggling to get to the bomb shelter, frightened children with their mother, the hungry for whom they cooked big pots of soup and those who needed clothes. One woman needed a pair of shoes sized 8½. Chiara prayed, 'Lord, give me a pair of shoes size 8½ for you in that poor person.' The shoes arrived.

The neighbour is seen as having Christ within, regardless of nationality or social background or faith. Focalare has grown and spread throughout the world. It has worked closely with other Christians and holds dialogue with world faiths.

The French Emmanuel community is charismatic and lay/religious/priestly with a focus on city mission. Members will take to the streets, stand outside churches and evangelize. They have great success with students and cope well with the disturbed and the drug dependent. Their literature abounds with moving testimonies of drug addicts and New Age practitioners who have found their way back to the church.

They gather families together each summer at Paray Le Monial, a centre in France, for a renewing retreat.

Dangers of enthusiasm?

Vatican II spoke of the need for both institution and charism. Ronald Knox, in his book *Enthusiasm* (1950), celebrates the structure and institutional nature of the church as a safeguard against extremism, but reminds the reader that it can also blind people to the dangers of routine and the need for ongoing renewal. The strength in the Catholic new ecclesial movements is the respect for the structure of the church and its abiding tradition, which anchors and earths their members in a wider tradition. Yet, there is room for flexibility and experimentation within different sub-cultures of 'postmodern' society.

Small-scale renewal movements might well be an important way ahead for Christianity in the twenty-first century. The English Cardinal Cormac Murphy O'Connor caused a stir in the press at the turn of the millennium. The headlines ran, 'Cardinal says Christianity is nearly vanquished in Britain'. His actual text was far more careful and positive. He made the valid point that the churches are in decline, that Britain (along with the West), is a secular, largely post-Christian society. The church is forced to the fringe of society. Yet, he predicted, 'there have been many worse periods in the life of the church. We are at the beginning of a new era... ' The way ahead is to have smaller but committed communities for prayer, worship and study that are vibrant in their faith. 'These small communities are the secret for the future of the Church.' Nominal believers might decline, and regular Sunday attendance might get lower for a season, but if such small groups catch a vision then they will evangelize afresh, whether these are emergent, fresh expressions, new communities with rules of life or parish groups.

Alpha

Small groups have been the secret of success for a pioneering course in basic Christianity that stemmed from the charismatic Anglican parish of Holy Trinity, Brompton, in London. This is presented by the Reverend Nicky Gumbel and exists on DVD and in book form. The idea is that small gatherings meet each week for a session but that they begin with a meal. This relaxed sharing time builds relationships and brings a degree of trust for people who might be wary of church. The sessions are presented in a light, lively manner with anecdotes and humour but there is a clear exposition of the gospel in fifteen units. This course is sometimes criticized as being too evangelical in tone, showing little awareness of other expressions of Christianity. It says next to nothing about liturgy or the sacraments, but it is effective, having spread out throughout the UK and over Europe and further afield. It also involves many different denominations, including the Catholic Church.

Return to orthodoxy?

Contrary to some of the emergent questioning, forms of orthodoxy are making a comeback in an uncertain age. This is seen in the desire of some Catholics to have the old Latin mass, now sanctioned for extraordinary use by Pope Benedict XVI in his *motu proprio* (his own ruling or motion) of 2007, or in a revival of membership to some religious communities, particularly women's orders on the continent. It is interesting to note the words of Father Benedict Groeschel of the Franciscan Friars of the Renewal in the USA, a new wing of the Franciscans, trying to return to the original rule: 'Many traditional religious orders are in confusion. Some are in a mediocre state. Only the orders which clearly engage in the proclamation of the gospel, with a fervent faith are "competitive", if you like.' He also saw their appeal in relevant, social action.

Another striking example is the rapid rise of charismatic or Pentecostal-style movements and groups around the world. They are reckoned to be the fastest growing form of Christianity in the early twenty-first century. Their theology is conservative and the Bible is taken almost literally. In the developing nations, traditional forms of faith are stronger than ever. There is a strong belief in the supernatural. Even more traditional groups can flourish; the Anglican Mothers' Union is thriving in Africa, for example, though it is beginning to decline in the UK. In Africa, it is functioning as the Mothers' Union was first envisaged, with the mainstay of membership based in young families. They wear their badges and uniforms with pride in the churches. A similar story is told in Baghdad where the lone Anglican church, St George's, is led by Canon Andrew White, a former archbishop's envoy to the Middle East. The Mothers' Union has a young membership, helping with cooking, food distribution and clothes for children in sometimes desperate and deprived circumstances.

There are revivalist movements gathering pace across the developing world where there is more openness to the supernatural and the reality of God. African charismatic churches have healing meetings and practise deliverance, in lands where evil spirits are feared in such a tribal culture. Latin American charismatics gather in the crowds with a similar 'signs and wonders' ministry, meaning that the message should be backed up by healings and miracles. Another intriguing development is the rise of missionaries to Europe and the USA from such nations. With the decline of faith in the secularized West, missionaries return to the homelands of their founding fathers to evangelize out of gratitude for what they have received. Thus Anglican African bishops oversee parishes in the USA who have broken away from ECUSA (Episcopal Church of the USA) over liberal morals and theology, including the ordination of women and practising homosexuals. Also, through the invitation of a local Baptist minister, Brazilian preachers assemble in the very British seaside resort of Bognor Regis, where there is now a lively Latin American musical tradition and a language school.

The persecuted church

The twentieth and twenty-first centuries have seen renewed persecution of Christians outside of the Western world. However, they have also seen unparalleled growth. China, to take another example, is seeing a rapid rise of new churches, 'house churches', even though some are fiercely persecuted. They have a committed membership in their thousands and many wish to be missionaries to different parts of the world, especially Muslim lands. Their 'Back to Jerusalem' movement seeks to see a massive evangelistic initiative converging upon the holy city from various sections of the globe.

Chinese house churches are radical in their discipleship and some do not fear martyrdom; they have been physically persecuted by the authorities on and off for years. One house church leader who has become well known in the West is Brother Yun. He had to leave China and travels telling the story of the believers there and preaching. His story was told in the best-selling book *The Heavenly Man*, the nickname he was given in prison because of his strong faith and the fact that he survived a prolonged fast. He fasted for weeks and confounded the authorities by staying alive when they should have given up all hope. One day, lying in his cell, he said that he felt the call of God telling him to get up and walk out. Doors were open and corridors were deserted, coincidentally, for that brief period. He walked out and was picked up by another believer who had felt that he had to drive his car outside the gate and wait.

Strong faith and the supernatural can also go together with persecution: Brother Yun's story is an example of this. China now has about thirty million Christians in a nation that tried to eradicate the faith in the Cultural Revolution of 1966. One reason for the rapid rise in conversions is the movement from rural areas to the cities in search of work. New technology and communication carries the message to a more open, seeking populace, separated from their village roots and old certainties. Included among China's Christians are an estimated five million Catholics. This community is divided between the 'underground' church which remains totally loyal to Rome, and the 'official' church, which is under the guidance of the government's Patriotic Association. The 'underground' members suffer relentless persecution with many clergy imprisoned and buildings destroyed. In recent years, diplomatic negotiations with the Vatican have helped to recognize 85 per cent of the bishops of the 'official' church. One bishop who has suffered imprisonment, Julius Jia Zhiguo, has been arrested at least eight times since 2004 and has spent over twenty years in prison. Bishop Jia, aged seventy in 2008, heads the diocese in the Hebei province, south of Beijing. This region has the highest concentration of Catholics. He lives a life where it seems perfectly normal to be in and out of police custody.

The few remaining communist countries often persecute Christians; in North Korea faith is practised in secret and owning a Bible can lead to execution. Cuba has relaxed much of its opposition and the church is growing whereas nearby Venezuela has anticlerical laws which have alarmed believers.

The Middle East also sees great times of persecution at the hands of extremist Muslims. Christians are sometimes seen as being pro-Western and supporting the invasion of Iraq. In Pakistan, for example, the Catholic archbishop of Lahore reported a rise of antipathy towards Christians in a country where they make up less than two per cent of the population.

There are killings and churches are fire-bombed.

In Gaza, a visit by Patriarch Sabbah of Jerusalem needed police protection to visit parishes, and priests have been abducted while driving to services. In Bethlehem, Christians now make up only one-quarter of the population whereas they made up three-quarters fifty years ago. There has been an emigration to more peaceful (and usually Western) climes. Whereas many used to leave for Lebanon, Muslim extremism and the Israel–Lebanon conflict in 2006 has seen the Christian community there dwindle by up to 40 per cent. This is also marked in Iraq where it is said that up to half of the Christian population have fled for their lives.

Militant Islam also affects Christians in parts of Africa under Islamic control, such as Nigeria. There, Christians can face physical persecution; ongoing violence in the Plateau State, for example, has claimed over 50,000 lives since 2001. Sometimes opposition can come in more peaceful ways such as the use of Saudi funds to implement economic projects in Sudan to encourage the conversion of Christian groups.

Talk of emergent and fresh expressions of worship and belief might seem far removed from these struggling, courageous communities: values and expectations differ around the world.

Where are Christians in the world today, and what does the future hold?

Of the world's Christians, about half are members of the Roman Catholic Church. The next largest groups are the Eastern Orthodox churches, and then the various Protestant groups. Of these, the Anglicans and then the Lutherans are the largest, though the greatest growth is now being seen in freer, evangelical, charismatic type congregations. This is the case worldwide.

The largest concentrations of Christians have been in Europe (both East and West), North and Latin America. Other areas have minority groups of Christians, whether in parts of Africa, the South Pacific islands or parts of the Middle East and Asia. This is still the case, though with the rise of secularism in the materialistic, consumer societies of the developed nations, belief is in decline and many people would claim to be 'Christian' only in a nominal sense. The developing nations are seeing a revival of faith and many large, vibrant churches. In these areas there is a greater openness to spirituality and a belief in the supernatural power of God. Healing prayers are popular, not only because of belief, but also because of less developed medical facilities and the poverty of some of the people.

If current trends continue world Christianity's centre of activity may well shift to the developing nations, as it shifted before from Syria, Palestine and North Africa in the early centuries. These were areas full of churches and great theologians – Augustine, Tertullian, Athanasius, Ephraim and so on. All this was displaced by the rise of Islam. Christians believe that God will protect his church until the end of time, but there is no guarantee for any particular denomination or geographical area. That depends upon a number of factors, socio-economic considerations, persecutions and, so believers feel, how faithful they are.

Timeline

1950s–1970s	Establishment of the key themes in postmodern philosophy
1970s	Charismatic renewal entered the mainline denominations, including the Roman Catholic Church. Formation of many of the new ecclesial movements (NEMs)
1990s–present	Rise of the emergent church in the USA and 'Fresh Expressions' in the UK

At a glance

- In a postmodern century with many lifestyles and beliefs, the church is trying to be flexible and creative. Many of the values espoused by postmodernism can be useful for the gospel, such as the role of the other and the poetic imagination.
- The emergent movement in the US tries smaller gatherings, embraces aspects of popular culture but also rethinks some of its evangelical roots and tends in a Liberal Protestant direction.
- Fresh Expressions in the UK experiments with style and meeting the needs of sub-cultures, but has not engaged theology in the same way.
- The new ecclesial movements (NEMs) in the Catholic Church form associations with rules of life and are involved in radical discipleship and service of others. Some are charismatic.
- There is a tension between charism and institution as new ways co-exist with traditional forms of church.
- Many also embrace traditional worship or doctrine in an age of postmodern change and flux, whether the Latin mass, fundamentalist charismatic churches or traditional religious orders.
- The developing world has a greater openness to the supernatural and also knows a great deal of persecution in some places. China, for example, has a rapidly growing number of Christians both in officially approved gatherings and in underground house churches or in the underground, unauthorized section of the Catholic Church.

Epilogue

'My name is Aviricus... '[1]

An inscription from an old Christian tomb in the Roman catacombs states:

> *My name is Aviricus, a disciple of the pure Shepherd who feeds the flocks of sheep on mountains and plains, who has great, all-seeing eyes. He taught me faithful Scriptures. To Rome he sent me. Everywhere I met with brethren. With Paul before me I followed, and Faith everywhere led the way and served food everywhere, the Fish from the spring – immense, pure, which the pure Virgin caught and gave to her friends to eat for ever, with good wine, giving the cup with the loaf... These things I, Aviricus, ordered to be written. I am truly seventy-two years old. Let him who understands these things, and everyone who is in agreement, pray for Aviricus.*

The sweep of Christian history has had many bleak points, ups and downs and rollercoaster rides of prejudice and hatred. Human beings show their failings all too easily. Behind all of this there is the tantalizing figure of Jesus of Nazareth, 'the pure Shepherd', hailed as God in the flesh by Christian believers.

Christians urge people to look to their master rather than their own failings. In amongst all the trials and persecutions down the ages, there is a gem of spirituality that shines forth, which still inspires people today. This moves some out of the secular scepticisms of Western society, gives courage and hope in the face of persecution in other parts of the world, and offers living faith in a supernatural reality. For others, it is a historical curiosity. How the history of the church will unfold remains unclear. Christians believe that whatever form it takes, God will be there – to quote the words of the risen Jesus in Matthew, 'I am with you always, even until the end of the age' (Matthew 28:20). Others will watch and wonder and wait to see what might happen. For all its faults and shortcomings, Christianity has been, and is, a great world religion that has contributed much to history, civilization, ethics and the arts.

Endnotes

1. Bamber Gascoigne, *The Christians*, London: Granada, 1978, pp. 27–28.

A Short Glossary of Key Terms

acceptatio   The moment when we are accepted by God through Christ.

aeon   A level of being in a hierarchy ascending to the high god in Gnostic thought. Can also mean an age, a symbolic period of time.

acta   The acts of the martyrs.

agapē   Love feast, the fellowship meal within which the early Christians held the eucharist.

Anabaptists   Those who believe in believer's baptism and discounted infant baptism as of no worth.

anathema   Condemned, left out, rejected. When anathemas are declared against other Christians they are said to be in error and are heretical.

Apollinarianism   Belief that there was no human soul in Jesus.

Arminian   Following Arminius who taught that God forsees who will be saved but desires that all should be.

autocephalos   A self-governing member of the Orthodox Churches.

canon   'Rule', or list of agreed books of Scripture.

catechumen   A learner, waiting to be baptized.

Cathar   Heretical group that revived Gnostic type ideas.

charismatic   One who believes in the supernatural gifts (charisms) of the Holy Spirit.

chrism   Scented oil used after baptism.

chrismation   Anointing with oil of chrism after baptism.

Confessing Church   The Christians who refused to accept German nationalism and anti-semitism during Hitler's time in office.

Congregational   A post Reformation denomination stressing that local congregations should run their chruches. This was very similar to Presbyterianism and the two movements in the UK joined in the United Reformed Church.

consubstantiation   Luther's idea that the substance of bread and wine remain in the eucharist, but the substance of the Body and Blood are united with them.

cosmological argument   The universe has a first cause, an unmoved mover.

demiurge   A go-between figure who made the world so that the high god would not be in direct touch with matter.

demythologizing   Stripping the Gospel of all supernatural content and putting existential values in their place.

diet   Assembly of the German rulers in the Reformation era.

docetism   The heresy that Jesus only appeared to be human.

dominical words   'This is my body… this is my blood.'

double predestination   God decrees who will be saved and who will be damned.

ecclesia   'Assembly', i.e. church.

election   Being chosen by God and saved by grace, though some argue by his decree and others just with his foreknowledge.

emergent   Experimental styles of worship and structures of Church in the USA.

enthusiasm   The term given to passionate, pietist religion in the seventeeth–eighteenth centuries.

episcopos   An overseer or bishop.

episcopal   Having bishops. The 'Episcopal Church' is the Anglican Church in various parts of the world, eg the USA.

eternally begotten   Meaning existing in relationship with the father from eternity. The eternal generation of the Persons of the trinity safeguards their full divinity.

eucharist   Thanksgiving, applied to the holy communion.

eutychianism   The belief that there is one unified nature in Christ, the God-Man.

filioque   The addition of 'and from the Son' to the Creed.

Fresh Expressions   Experimental worship and targeting particular interest groups in the UK.

gnosis/Gnosticism   An eclectic theological and philosophical system that mixed pagan and Greek ideas into Christianity.

Great Awakening   The revival that swept the American Colonies in the mid eighteenth century and influenced the Wesleyian revival in England.

hesychast   'Silence', a meditative, mystical strand within Orthodoxy that uses the Jesus Prayer.

hilasterion   Either 'propitiation' or 'expiation'.

homoiousios   'Of like or similar substance'.

homoousios   'Of the same substance'.

hypostases   Extensions of divine being and power at work in the world.

hypostatic union   A union of the divine and human essences or substances in Jesus Christ. Such that neither is absorbed by the other. Jesus is thus seen as truly God and truly human.

Judaizer   A Jewish Christian who tried to make Gentile converts into full Jews by observing the ritual laws of the Torah such as circumcision.

justification by faith   The sinner needs the grace of God to be saved and cannot earn this by works. However, good works should be the sign of a genuine conversion and an 'infusio' of grace into the soul.

kiss of peace   Sharing the peace before the eucharist.

icon   A holy image that is seen as a 'window into heaven'.

iconostasis   A screen at the front of an Orthodox Church covered with icons.

Independents   Christians in the UK who avoided state interference in their faith and worship after the Reformation.

indulgences   A partial or total declaration of release from the temporal punishments of sin.

infusio   Medieval term for the infusion of saving, sanctifying grace into the soul.

institution narrative   The words of Jesus at the Last Supper.

liberation theology   Radical theologians from the developing World, particularly Latin America have argued for a bias to the poor and a need to challenge capitalist society.

liturgy   Eucharistic rite of the Orthodox Churches.

Logos   The Word of God, Reason, the creative power of principle.

Lollards   'Babblers' a nickname for the followers of Wyclif.

Manichees   Followers of Manes who taught a form of Gnosticism whereby matter was evil.

Mar Thoma   Indian Christians who trace their heritage back to the Apostle Thomas.

martyr   One who witnesses, especially one who gives his or her life for the faith.

mendicant   Wandering preachers or friars.

Mission-shaped church   An Anglican buzz-word for targeting particular groups and accepting that there is no single community.

modalism   The belief that the Persons as like modes, roles or masks of the one God.

Modernists   A Catholic movement in the nineteenth/early twentieth centuries that adapted catholic faith to liberal ideas.

monophysite   One nature in the incarnate Christ, a union of God and man.

monothelite   The belief that there was only one will in Christ (God's).

new ecclesial movements   New communities and methods of evangelism in the Catholic Church.

nous   The intellect, or the 'world-soul' in neo-Platonism.

ordinal   The rite of Ordination.

paradosis   Tradition, that which is handed down.

pelagianism   The belief that we can earn forgiveness without the grace of God by one's own efforts. Whether this was actually taught by Pelagius himself is a moot point.

pentarchy   The establishment of the five Patriarchates.

Pentecostal   One who has experienced the 'baptism in the Holy Spirit' and believes in the gifts of the Holy Spirit.

pleroma   The fullness, meaning the full reality of the High God and not a lesser divine being.

post-evangelical   People with evangelical spirituality and roots who have moved beyond the confines of that tradition and are exploring further.